"I have known and have worked with Richard Broom for well over ten years. I know him to be a person who takes pride in helping other people who are recovering from the disease of addiction, and I don't know anyone who does it better. In particular, he has helped numerous police and corrections officers who have remained in contact with him for years after getting clean and sober. Richard works his own recovery program, which gives him a spirituality that can only come from being to hell and coming back. He is among the few people I would trust with anything, including my life. At some point during these past ten plus years I learned about Richard's personal history. I learned that while under the influence of his own disease he killed another human being: That he spent years in prison and will never be free of the consequences of what occurred in an alcoholic blackout. Yet, I believe in every word of his story, his redemption, and would still trust him with my life and with the life of anyone close to me. His story is truly heroic and deserves to be shared with the world."

—Michael Wiener, Ph.D.
Executive Director, Seaside Palm Beach

"Richard Broom has produced a great read. *Cocked and Loaded* is more than a person's journey into recovery; it presents a powerful message of resurrection and redemption. I know Richard Broom. I see him and work alongside him every month. The message he brings to clients at Behavioral Health of the Palm Beaches incorporates the spiritual message of transformation and hope found in this book. Few alcoholics committed a murder in a blackout; even fewer were able to write about it. *Cocked and Loaded* grabs you from the first page and reads real through every page. I recommend this book to everyone."

Booth

COCKED

— AND —

LOADED

RICHARD BROOM

Health Communications, Inc.
Deerfield Beach, Florida

www.hcibooks.com

Library of Congress Cataloging-in-Publication Data

Broom, Richard, 1946-
    Cocked & loaded / Richard Broom.
        p. cm.
    ISBN-13: 978-0-7573-1367-7
    ISBN-10: 0-7573-1367-1
    1. Broom, Richard, 1946-   2. Recovering alcoholics—United States—
Biography.   3. Twelve-step programs.   4. Alcoholics Anonymous.
5. Prisoners—United States—Biography.   I. Title.   II. Title: Cocked and loaded.
HV5068.B796 2010
362.292092—dc22
[B]

                                                                        2009044572

Publisher: Health Communications, Inc.
        3201 S.W. 15th Street
        Deerfield Beach, FL 33442–8190

Cover photo ©Sir Eagle, Fotolia.com
Cover design by Larissa Hise Henoch
Interior design and formatting by Lawna Patterson Oldfield

To my daughter Kathryn,
who stuck by me through the years
of turmoil and who harassed me for ten years
until I wrote this book, because she
believes it will help people.

Acknowledgments

T O ALL THE TWELVE-STEP PROGRAM MEMBERS throughout the world who brought meetings into institutions—many thanks to each of you.

And special thanks to: Jennifer Brady Cotter, who helped me immensely in making this book readable and without whom this book would never have been completed; my editor, Michele Matrisciani, for the guidance, book cover concept, and book title, as well as to René Reese, whose communication skills via the computer made my life easier; Dr. Donald Mullaney, my employer and friend, who encouraged me and helped me contact the publisher; and Doe Thornton, who put up with me for the sixteen months it took to write this book.

Chapter One

THE HOT FLORIDA SUN SHOT THROUGH THE BLINDS, piercing my brain as I came to. Bleary-eyed I gazed around the room trying to figure out where the hell I was. It was July 5, 1982. I was 36 years old, and hanging from the bedpost was my .44 Magnum in its western-style holster. For some reason, I was more uneasy about why I had my gun with me than about whose bed I was in.

The curtains were drawn, and I lay alone in the darkness with an impending sense of doom, trying to remember how I ended up celebrating the good old Fourth of July. Foggy memories of the earlier part of the night came to me, and I relaxed a bit as I recalled shooting my gun off into the night sky. *That's right,* I thought. *I was just entertaining some of the lads and lassies at the Tender Trap Saloon by showing off my own brand of fireworks.*

A sudden knock at the door interrupted my thoughts and Karen's weathered face appeared. "Oh no, not her . . ." I muttered under my breath, pissed at myself for winding up with Karen again. I didn't even like her.

"Dick, grab the damn phone. Someone wants to talk to you," she snapped and slammed the door shut.

After fumbling around in the shadows, I finally found the phone. My good friend Cherie was on the other end of the line. "Hey, darlin'! How's it going?" I asked.

"Dick, what the hell are you doing?" Her voice trembled. "Don't you know that the police are looking for you? You shot two people last night!"

After a brief pause, I quietly asked, "I what?" Despite what she said, I had no recollection of what had happened. All I knew was that I must have really screwed up this time. Desperate to put the pieces of the puzzle together, I tried to focus on what Cherie was saying.

I lit a smoke, lay back in bed, and listened as she nervously told me about what went down in the Tender Trap—a dumpy topless bar where I used to work. I had quit that job over a month before because I couldn't take the place anymore. The only reason I even worked there was because I was able to drink ten to twenty beers a night for free during my shift. Apparently, I had plenty in me by midnight when I popped two guys right in the bar.

"That's all I really know, honey. I wish I had more to tell you," said Cherie sadly.

"I'm sure I'll hear more," I groaned. "Thanks for filling me in."

"Be safe," she whispered and she was gone.

My first move after hanging up with Cherie was to venture out to the kitchen to find a drink so I could think. I wasn't too picky—anything would do—but I was comforted when I dug into the fridge and found a small supply of Old Milwaukee I'd purchased the night before.

Once armed with a beer, I eased into the living room and plopped down next to Karen on the couch. "So, uhhh . . ." I stammered. "Do you know what the heck happened last night?"

"You shot two guys, idiot," Karen snarled, not even taking her eyes off the TV. "You really did it this time. You're lucky my sister is out of town and you have a place to figure out what the hell you're gonna do."

I sat in silence but my head was pounding. I tried to quiet it down and recall any details from the night before. Who did I shoot? Why did I do it? But nothing came to me. Blackouts weren't new to me. They had been happening for many years, and over the past eighteen months I was having them three or four times a week. I knew that no matter how hard I tried, I wasn't going to remember anything, so I hopped on the phone and started calling around to see if anyone could fill me in on what had happened.

By beer number three, I had called a bunch of people and hadn't found out anything. I realized that it was time to evaluate my options. I could call a lawyer I knew in Fort Lauderdale and turn myself in. I could also try to sneak back to the house I shared with my friend Bart and take off in the "company car," or I could just kill myself and end the goddamn drama already. I had half-heartedly tried to do it a bunch of times over the past year. Hell, just three days ago I'd had the same .44 Magnum in my mouth, hammer cocked.

As I considered my options that fateful afternoon, another idea popped into my head. I could make the cops kill me—commit suicide by police. Weren't they looking for me at this very minute? Maybe I could even take a couple of them with me and go out in a real blaze of glory.

I decided to call Paul the attorney first. If that didn't work out, then I would find a way to get the car and take off. And if the cops caught up with me beforehand—screw it; let 'em kill me.

After grabbing another brew, I pulled out my wallet and rifled through scraps of papers with women's phone numbers, pictures of my kids, my social security card, and rolling papers. I eventually found Paul's card and dialed.

"Hello, this is Mr. Cohen's office," a cheery woman's voice answered the phone.

"I need to talk to Paul," I said.

"Oh, sorry. He is out of the office today. Since the Fourth of July was on a Sunday, everyone has off today for the holiday. Would you like to leave a message?"

"Can you get it to him right away?" I asked politely, trying to stay calm.

"Well, he's on the golf course today, sir. But I'm sure he'll get back to you at his earliest convenience."

"I'll guess I'll try to get back to him tomorrow. Enjoy the holiday," I said sweetly while giving her the finger. "That's a hell of a way to run a law firm," I growled to Karen after slamming down the phone. She just rolled her eyes and went to take a shower.

With that option off the table, I tried to figure out how to get to the car parked in front of the little shitbox I called home. The police probably had the place staked out already, so the car and the money I had buried in plastic bags around the house would be impossible to get to.

The only option left was to grab another beer. Once that was polished off and Karen was polished up, I coaxed her to head out to a couple of the local watering holes. To keep under the radar, we went to a bunch of new places where we wouldn't be known.

All afternoon, I repeated my rationale for not being able to turn myself in without a lawyer. "Are you kidding me? I know what will happen to me. I've already had my face smashed into a sergeant's desk and been whacked on the head by troopers with a billy club. No way am I going in there without my own cavalry." Of course, I failed to mention why I might have deserved this kind of treatment.

At each bar, Karen listened half-heartedly to my pitch as she chain-smoked and tossed down her scotch and soda. She would nod her head or occasionally chime in and say something like, "Yeah, you'd be crazy to go in alone." The truth was she couldn't have cared less whether or not they kicked my ass. She just wanted me to shut up.

Hours later we stumbled back to Karen's sister's house, and I continued my drinking and thinking routine. At the same time I realized that I would run out of beer soon—there were only seven left—and Karen said she wanted to get some grub. "Here's a couple of bucks. Grab me a case of OM and some smokes. Go get yourself some chow, too," I said as I tossed her some cash. The screen door slammed behind her before I could mutter, "Thanks for listening to me."

Alone, the gravity of the situation began to sink in. Lying on the couch, I slammed two more beers. I closed my eyes and nervously thought to myself, *How the hell did I get here? What am I going to do? What's going to happen to me? I need to get out of this house and out of this town.*

An hour later I came to. I didn't wake up anymore, I just came to. Typically, I would be unconscious for three or four hours until I needed a beer again. When I walked to the fridge and realized that there were still only five beers stocked in the fridge, it hit me that Karen wasn't back yet. Maybe she got scared and took off. The truth was that would be a relief. My only problem with her not coming back was that I was going to run out of beer soon.

Needing a partner in crime, I decided to call my friend Martha after pulling her number out of my wallet. "Hey, girl. What's shakin'?"

"Dick! Oh my god! The cops came by here looking for you. What are you going to do?" she cried.

"I'm gonna meet you at the bar on the corner of Forest Hill Boulevard and we're going to enjoy a couple of cocktails. How does that sound to you?"

"Are you okay?" she asked hesitantly.

"I'm fine and I'll be better when I see you," I said and hung up before she had a chance to say no. I immediately felt a sense of calm.

Martha had her act together and was one person who would actually be able to help me to come up with a successful game plan.

With a skip in my step I gathered up the important things in my life and tossed them into a brown paper bag: three cans of beer, my holster, and the Sturm and Ruger .44-Mag Super Black Hawk revolver. After putting the last cold beer into a coolie, I grabbed my bag of treasures and walked to the front windows. I peered out through the blinds looking for anything resembling the police. The coast looked clear and I headed out in to the hot July night. The sun hadn't set yet, but there were clouds on the horizon. It looked as if a storm was getting ready to roll in.

As I walked out the door, I began to think that things might actually turn out all right in the long run. I was finally getting out of Palm Beach County to live a life on the run. It was the beginning of a new adventure. Walking down the driveway with my goodies under one arm and my beer in hand, I noticed two men in camouflage outfits crawling along the lakefront house about 120 feet away.

Holy shit! That's some blackout. Last thing I remember it was July 5, and now it's Halloween, I chuckled to myself. *And I thought it was bad when I started drinking in Fort Lauderdale and woke up in Charleston, South Carolina.*

Suddenly I heard someone shout, "Freeze!"

"Freeze? Hell, it's like 100 degrees out here," I cracked and kept walking.

The same voice yelled, "Freeze, Broom, or I'll blow your fucking head off!"

This, of course, caught my attention and I turned around to find the two trick-or-treaters pointing shotguns at me, plus more cops bursting out of the bushes. All of them were yelling, "Get down on the ground! Drop the bag! Drop the thing in your right hand!" For a moment I considered pulling the gun out of the bag so I could take at least one of them with me. But as their barrage of threats continued, I dropped the bag and got down—but only after I drank the rest of my beer.

As I lay on the ground, feeling the shotguns on the back of my neck and on my lower spine, I took a deep breath and released a long, loud sigh from the depths of my soul. "You're glad we caught you, Broom. You want to get this off your conscience, right?" presumed one of the cops.

Nope, that wasn't it. I was thinking I wasn't going to be having a drink for a long time.

As I was cuffed and shoved into the back of a waiting police car, I vaguely registered the cameras and bright lights capturing the entire scene. I would later make it on to the eleven o'clock news. Lucky me, I was about to get my fifteen seconds of fame.

Chapter Two

THE CAMERAS AND LIGHTS FADED INTO THE DISTANCE as we headed off to the Sheriff's station. As we passed the airport I watched a plane take off. If I had had my shit together, I might have been on a plane to Brazil. But I got drunk instead and was stuck listening to Deputy Dimwit brag about taking me down to the older detective grinning in the front seat.

Upon arrival at the station, I was handcuffed to a chair next to the detective's desk. Everything started off friendly. The detective was a guy in his late forties, overweight, with a receding hairline and a New York accent. I guessed he was another one of those double dippers—collecting a pension from a gig in New York while working toward getting another one from Florida.

"So, where are you from?" he asked while he took his coat off and loosened his tie.

"New York."

"No way! Me too. I have a lot of family up there still. I go up for the holidays now and then, but I'm glad to escape the winters. Where in New York did you live?"

"Around Albany." I wondered how long we were going to have to make small talk.

"What brought you down here?" he asked, as if we were just two guys chatting it up at the bar.

"The same reasons as you—warm weather, cocktails on the beach . . ." I said.

"Chicks in bikinis year-round. I hear ya," he chuckled. "So . . . any chance you're Italian?"

"Yeah, my grandfather was from Sicily," I lied. The truth was that Grandpa Al was from Sicily, but he was just my stepgrandfather on my mother's side. I was really German.

"Sicily, huh? So that's how it is." The detective smiled, snickered, and started to roll up his sleeves. Obviously he was looking for some sort of mob connection and thought the shootings were a hit job.

"Yeah, that's how it is," I said. At that moment, I realized that I was just digging myself into a deeper hole. I wasn't sure how much he knew, but I recognized it was time to clam up. "I think it's time for me to talk to a lawyer."

In the blink of an eye, good cop became bad cop. He leaned over, got right in my face, and growled, "Oh, is that what you want, Broom? You think you're hot shit, don't you? Listen asshole, I've been dealing with losers like you for a long time and you better start talking now or I'm gonna lock you up."

"Gee, like that's not going to happen an hour from now anyway. Go ahead, jerk off, lock me up!" I snapped back, not the least surprised at the sudden change in his attitude.

After that friendly exchange and another fruitless call to Paul Cohen's answering service, I was off to the hoosegow. Since I was still pretty wasted, going to the county jail was a blur. I vaguely remember trading in my cowboy boots, dress shirt, and jeans for a jazzy orange jumpsuit—after the delightful experience of being strip-searched.

Entering the depths of the old Palm Beach County jail felt like boarding a submarine. There were five floors of cells, each one made solely of concrete and metal. The cell I went into had a couple picnic tables with about twenty guys watching TV. Off to the side were five cells with beds bolted to the walls. They weren't really beds in the conventional sense, just metal slabs with inch-thick mattresses. As rough as they were, you'd be lucky to get a bed on a busy night; many times all you had was the floor.

Shortly after entering the cell, the eleven o'clock news came on and I was the lead story. One of the lads in the cell yelled out, "No way! That's that guy over there!" The screen showed me being tossed into the back of the police car with a woman on the screen reporting, " . . . finally captured the main suspect from the Fourth of July shooting at the notorious Tender Trap Saloon in Palm Springs. Stay tuned for more information on this breaking story."

The other guys in the cell gathered around the TV to celebrate my fifteen seconds of fame. I was an instant celebrity and, pathetically, I felt a sense of pride for being a big shot in the cesspool.

For the first couple of hours in the jail, I had different guys come up to tell me about the injustice being imposed on their innocent souls. They shared their sordid tales of how they were framed; then they shook their heads in disbelief and wistfully hoped against hope that the truth would set them free. As other people entered the cell, I watched as they told the same stories again, and began to realize that they were simply rehearsing their lies for the courtroom.

For the rest of the night I pretended to watch TV while trying to figure out what the hell I was going to do. I'd left my message with the golf-aficionado lawyer in Fort Lauderdale who got me off in the past on a false arrest for drug trafficking, but I still had no idea what was going on. I had so many questions racing through my head. *What did I do? When was my bail hearing? What was going to happen to me?*

To make things worse, the booze was beginning to wear off.

After finally dozing off for a few hours, I was woken up for break-fast. Throughout the meal there was a flurry of fast-talking and trades that made me dizzy. Outside the cell I saw a guard flipping through the newspaper, and the headline caught my eye. There, on the cover of the paper, was a photo of me in cuffs headed into the cop car. The caption read: *Police Arrest Cowboy Hit Man!*

"Jesus Christ, " I mumbled to myself.

How was it possible that everyone in Palm Beach knew more-about why I was locked up than I did? The answers were right there, just outside the cage, but beyond my reach. I was the one stuck behind bars, but left in the dark about what had happened. Maybe I was better off; maybe I didn't want to know.

As the morning progressed, I started swinging back and forth between having the chills and then the sweats. Perhaps they were caused by my impending sense of doom or by the revolting smells emanating from the communal toilet—always within a few feet of me. In retrospect, I was most likely going through detox, but I wouldn't have recognized it at that point in my life. It had been years since I had sobered up. The only time I stopped drinking was when I passed out.

Later that day I was shackled from head to foot and transported in a van to the courthouse for my arraignment. After waiting for a couple hours to see the judge, a deputy finally came to escort me to the courtroom. On the ride up in the elevator he got a call. After hanging up, he pressed the down button, sending us back from where we came. He then turned to me and said, "You're not gonna be arraigned today. One of the victims just died." My stomach sank along with the elevator as I realized that now I was going to be charged with murder.

Upon my return to the jail, I tried to come to grips with what was going on. Sitting in a state of shock in the corner of the cell, I

numbly watched the other prisoners revel in the ceremonial straining of the "buck." Referred to as "hooch" in northern prisons, buck
is made of a combination of any fruit or fruit cocktail, sugar from
the morning coffee and cereal, bread for the yeast, fruit juices, and
water. The concoction is placed in a huge garbage bag and left to fer-
ment for about seven days until the sugar turns to alcohol. The new
batch was ready today, and the prisoners were eagerly straining it
through their shirts and underwear, anticipating the potent drink
that was around 15 to 20 percent alcohol.

There they were, scooping it up with plastic cups and passing
them around to the crew. The lads progressively got louder, sillier,
and pretty damn drunk. They were quite jovial, almost like kids on
a sugar high after hitting the candy store. I couldn't believe it. Just
yesterday I was thinking I wouldn't be able to drink again for a long
time, and here I was in the county jail with five gallons of booze in
front of me.

When the houseman eventually offered me a glass, I surprised
myself by passing on it, saying I wasn't feeling well. While the buck
may have made me feel better, it was crystal clear that this was what
had got me here in the first place. I didn't want to drink again—at
least not that day.

All night I tossed and turned. This was my second night locked
up and I began to feel trapped. I had been picked up by the cops
before, but I was always bailed out within a couple of hours. Now,
everything seemed so surreal. There was no escaping the thought
that this might become my new reality.

On July 7 I returned to the courthouse to be arraigned for first-
degree murder and first-degree attempted murder. As I headed into
the courtroom, I had no idea what to expect. My only plan was to
get bailed out, make some quick cash through whatever means necessary, and then take off for somewhere I couldn't be extradited, like
Brazil.

Unfortunately, things don't always go according to plan. The judge ordered no bond, which meant I would have to go back to county jail until the trial or a bond hearing. I did see Cohen along with his partner in the back of the courtroom, so when the judge asked me where my lawyer was, I could at least say, "He's here, but not retained yet."

The judge then asked, "What's your plea?"

"Not guilty," I said defiantly.

Back in the holding cell, waiting to go back to jail, Cohen paid me a visit. "Don't worry, Dick. We can take care of this for you."

"Good. How much are you going to need?" I asked pensively.

"Well, it's a tough case and will take a lot of work. It'll probably run you around $25,000."

"Uh, okay. I'll get back to you on it," I said, knowing full well that there wasn't a chance in hell I could cover it. I only had five grand, including what was buried in the plastic bags in my backyard. I tried to hit up my family, and my grandmother said she would try to help, but $25,000 was impossible.

A couple days later a guard came to the cell and said, "Broom, come down here." I followed him, with no clue where or why he was taking me. He brought me to an office where two men in suits were sitting behind a table waiting to talk to me.

"Nice to meet you, Mr. Broom," said one of the men.

"Nice to meet you. Who are you?" I asked.

"My name is Mr. Abrahms and this is Mr. Feinstein. We are public defenders assigned to your case by the State of Florida."

"Oh, I didn't know what was going on when I came up here," I explained.

"Sorry about that," apologized Feinstein. "There seems to be a real lack of communication around here. We just want you to know that we will give this case everything we've got. It's a very interesting case."

"How so?" I asked.

"Well . . . most of the witness reports are sketchy. There may be mitigating factors that could impact the charges—not to mention the problem with your paperwork."

"What problem?" I interrupted.

"There was a mistake on the paperwork that says you were arrested on July 6. That's impossible because you were in jail on that date. These kinds of technicalities often get people off."

I leaned back and grinned. Not only were these guys free, but they were intelligent, too. Maybe there was hope after all.

Chapter Three

FOR THE NEXT FEW DAYS IT FELT AS IF MY BRAIN WAS bouncing off my skull. Detoxing in jail while coming to grips with the fact that you might be introduced to "Ol' Sparkie," the electric chair at Florida State Prison, might be considered the mother of all hangovers.

On top of that, my fellow inmates immediately squashed my newfound hope in the public defenders. Apparently, the "public offenders"—as their grateful clients affectionately called them—were usually completely useless. While I knew that inmates weren't always the most reliable sources, I also realized that even if Feinstein and Abrahms were sharp, hardworking public servants, they had so many cases that it would be unlikely they'd have the time to be the heroes I so desperately needed.

In light of this revelation, it was time to come up with a Plan B. Upon the expert advice of my insightful compadres, I would hire a real lawyer, but not until the public defender's office had their private investigators dig up some dirt on the victim. They could find out information for free that would otherwise cost me five grand if

a regular lawyer hired them. I was convinced that the victim couldn't
have been a model citizen if he was hanging out at a sketchy topless
bar after midnight on the Fourth of July. So I decided to string along
Feinstein and Abrahms until they got the scoop on who this guy was.

In the meantime I would hunt around for a good criminal lawyer
and beg my family for money to pay him. It wasn't long before I
started getting lots of mail from old friends and acquaintances. One
of the first letters I got was from my longtime fraternity brother,
Howie, now a big shot at one of the New York State worker unions.
I was surprised to hear from him, but appreciated his heartfelt com-
passion for my plight—that is, until he got to the real reason he had
contacted me. He wanted to know how it felt to kill someone. Of
course, I got back to him right away and began by apologizing to
him for not being able to give him a cheap thrill. I explained that I
didn't remember how it felt to murder someone because I was in a
blackout, but if he really wanted to know, he should go out and kill
someone himself. For some reason, he didn't write back to let me
know how that worked out.

"You'll get a lot of mail at first, but it'll slow down to a trickle once
you satisfy everyone's curiosity about what life is like on the inside,"
explained Chuck, a fellow inmate who seemed to be the brains of the
cell block. A well-educated guy, he looked like a college professor
who needed a haircut. Unfortunately, he was also a federal inmate
awaiting trial for crack cocaine charges. Of course, he was innocent.
Everyone in there was charged with crimes that hadn't *really*
happened, or else they were overcharged—meaning the state made
sure they copped to a lesser charge so they wouldn't go to trial. For
instance, take Bob, a six-foot, seven-inch Polish guy from Detroit
who was in for strong-armed robbery. In his case, after buying and
swilling a bottle of wine from 7-11, he filled the bottle up with water
and returned it, complaining that it tasted like shit. Of course it
tasted like shit; it was the kind of wine that had never seen a grape

and came with a twist-off cap. His scam worked the first, second, and third time he pulled it, but the fourth time he came stumbling back into the store, his ranting and raving scared the store clerk, and he was promptly arrested for assault. Bob had a prior record and no money, so he copped a plea and got three years. It was a classic case of the "just-us" system—if you're among the chosen people who have the money, you can get off. Everyone else is stuck in the slammer.

A month into my incarceration, I decided that I needed to escape somehow, even if it was just mentally. It was the only way to survive. After talking to my most experienced cell buddies, I concluded that I should try to get my hands on some psychotropic meds, something that would take me out of this hellhole into la-la land; in order to get them, however, I had to appear crazy. I set out to do this immediately.

The following morning, I rolled my oatmeal into a fat cigar shape, poured coffee over it, and let it dry. As a finished product, it looked quite strikingly like feces. At the next meal, I snagged a piece of wax paper. Later on in my cell, I heard the nurse walking through the cell block distributing meds. As she approached our cell, I placed the wax paper on top of the water in the toilet next to the wall of bars. Then I carefully placed the cigar poo on top of the paper. When the nurse was in front of me, I growled at her to get her attention, reached down into the toilet bowl, pulled out the turd look-alike and started ravenously eating it, smearing some on my lips and face.

That evening, without ever seeing a doctor, I received my first dose of Thorazine (a psychiatric drug most popular for treating schizophrenia). I slept fairly well, dreaming many strange dreams.

The following morning, I got my second dose and was spaced out all day. I lost all motor control and could barely walk, talk, or even feed myself. It felt like an out-of-body experience and I didn't like it.

After trying one more dose that afternoon, I stopped taking the pills. Later on I found out that psychotropic drugs mellowed out people who were psychotic and, apparently, I wasn't psychotic—even though I acted like a psychopath when I was drunk.

Over the next few weeks, I went through a number of motion hearings, including one to deny me bond. Based on word of mouth on the inside, I hunted down several different lawyers. We had a simple interview during which I would ask two questions: How much? and Can you get me off? I finally selected a young hot shot, Mike Silverstein, who had won a bunch of big cases already. I liked his personality; he wasn't an egomaniac or overly slick, and his price was right.

Most of the money came from my grandmother. Originally my father said that he would mortgage the house to get me out, but then he decided that his money would be better spent on my sister's college education. Somehow I scraped together the money to hire Silverstein and another hearing was set before the "fast and speedy trial" was to begin. In order to be "fast and speedy," the State has to prosecute you within 180 days of your arraignment. The defense has the right to ask for a continuance, which we did so that Mike would have time to prepare for the trial.

The wheels were finally in motion. The public defenders were cut loose, but only after their private investigators found out that the murder victim was a strong-arm extortionist who would bully people out of their money. Silverstein also interviewed over a dozen witnesses to the crime. As I read the depositions, I was finally able to piece together what happened that fateful night.

Of particular interest was a deposition from a guy named Red whom I knew only by his nickname until I read his report. Red was a little guy with a big mouth—a typical Florida redneck, hence the nickname. He was a handyman with a wife and kids, but somehow found time to be a regular at the bar and was an alcoholic like me.

According to Red, I was already there when he arrived some time in the early evening. It seemed like I had been drinking for a while and was acting funny. Shortly after he sat down next to me, I pulled out a large revolver to show off and he told me to put it away—which I did for the moment.

As I read his deposition, I remembered that two months before the crime, Red came in to the bar to show me his .357 Sturm-Ruger Blackhawk model. It was close to the same make and model as mine. My guess was that that was why I brought my gun it into the bar on the Fourth of July, to show him that mine was bigger than his.

The night wore on and we continued drinking. Around midnight a couple of men came into the topless bar and started raising hell. One of them started pushing around one of the dancers. According to one witness, the pusher spit at me and another witness said I told the pusher that "I oughta take you out!" Red reported that I then stood up, pulled the gun out of my waistband, swung it around, and aimed it over the middle of the bar where all the chaos was. Red tried to grab my wrist to stop me, but the gun fired and shot a man who had nothing to do with the altercation. Red stated that I pulled my arm away from him and fired a couple of rounds toward the middle of the bar. At that point he took off.

Another deposition reported that after I fired twice over the bar, I walked around it and shot the troublemaker right in the ass. I then went back to my seat, finished my beer, and left the scene. Looking back, I guess with my twisted mind-set I was trying to give an asshole a new one.

It was so surreal; the story was all new to me. Not only was the tale itself troubling, but so was the fact that it didn't jar my memory in any way. Nothing came back to me, even after reading all of these depositions.

At this point, I knew it must have been me who committed the crime. Silverstein wanted to say that the victim had a gun. The truth was that no one said he didn't have a gun and I briefly considered this strategy. But it would be hard to fabricate something when I honestly had no idea what even happened except for what other people had to say. Plus, I didn't want to have to lie any longer.

The bottom line was that the depositions didn't change anything. I was still awaiting trial for first-degree murder and first-degree attempted murder. I was in constant fear of what fate had in store for me. *Am I heading to the electric chair? Will I be in prison for the rest of my life? Will I ever have a chance at a decent life?*

Always on edge, it took all my strength not to turn my rage on someone else. Instead, I turned it inward and slipped into a state of depression. I guess that was better than having a fight. Silverstein warned me to avoid any violence in jail. I defended myself when necessary, but somehow kept my rage at bay when confronted with a conflict. I was surprised that I was able to keep my cool; I had never seemed to be able to do that before.

During this time, there were weekly Twelve-Step recovery meetings held in jail that my buddy Bob, a biker from Detroit, would go to. One day he asked my why I wouldn't.

"I don't feel like being chained up to go to some stupid meeting," I muttered. Every time you were moved to someplace inside or outside of the building you were handcuffed and chained up to a bunch of other people. I added, "I've never been to one before. Why should I start now?".

"Because you're a goddamn alcoholic! " Bob laughed. "Plus, since you committed your crime under the influence, the judge might look more favorably on you if you look like you're trying to clean up your act."

"Screw the judge—I don't care what he thinks. I wouldn't go to a meeting even if he told me to go," I boasted.

"Okay, tough guy. Hopefully, one of these days you'll get over yourself and wind up at a meeting," Bob said as he shook his head and walked away.

"Bullshit!" I yelled, not sure why I was so angry.

Chapter Four

OR THE NEXT COUPLE OF MONTHS, MAIL CONTINUED to come in from long lost friends and acquaintances. However, almost all of the letters were written out of morbid curiosity about what life was like on the inside. Everyone would ask the same damn question: "How do you stand it?" My only answer was that I had no choice. There were times when I felt as if I couldn't take one more minute of it. I wanted to run across the cell headfirst into the steel bars and split my head open . . . but those moments came and went. Most of the time I tried to keep my head together, get along with the rest of the men in the cell, and watch my back.

But I sank deeper and deeper into the insane world of my fellow inmates, and I became more and more desperate to keep a connection to the outside world. Unfortunately, as Chuck had predicted, my mail began to dwindle. Once in a while, I'd get a couple of letters from old friends, like my fraternity brother Bob and my buddy Don who later became a counselor. They were among the few who weren't looking for horror stories, but who actually wanted to know how I was doing. However, most people simply lost interest. My friend George's wife, Olivia, actually wrote to tell me that she couldn't stand hearing about the conditions in jail anymore, and she would not be writing to me again. She even told me to leave them alone—so I did.

The only mail I could count on getting regularly consisted of Catholic Mass cards from my grandmother. Of course, at this point, I had little faith in anything. Early on in my stay at County, I said my foxhole prayers, begging God to get me out trouble. After a couple days of praying to get out of the charges, to no avail, I asked God just to get me out of jail on bail and then I would take it from there. That didn't work either. Since God wouldn't give me a break, I decided to ask his counterpart for some help. After trying old Lucifer for a week or two without any luck, I gave up on it altogether.

Months went by and my lawyer continued preparing for my case. After interviewing me and finding out that I was hit over the head by numerous types of blunt objects such as beer mugs, bottles, and police sticks, he decided that I should have my brain checked for damage or injury. So he set up an EEG test to measure my brain waves and look for any physiological damage.

Before the test started, my brain was wired up to a machine. Then a doctor came in, handed me a jigger-sized plastic cup filled with a liquid, and said, "Drink this, Mr. Broom."

Ten minutes after I slammed it, the doc looked into my eyes and gave me another cup to swill. I started to feel relaxed and even chuckled a couple times as I waited another ten minutes with the doctor. When the time was up, he looked into my eyes again. Stunned, he said, "I can't believe it. You need another shot of liquid Valium!"

I laughed and tossed down the third cup. Finally really relaxed, I was administered the test. When it was over, the doctor shook his head and said, "I never had to give anyone three shots of Valium before. You must have one hell of a tolerance, Broom."

As the guards escorted me out of the room, I grinned and asked, "Any chance I could have a six-pack of that shit to go?" The doctor laughed along with the guards and I felt great for the rest of the afternoon.

About a week later I was pulled out of the block and brought in to meet with Silverstein. As soon as I sat down he said, "Well, I don't know if this is good or bad news, but your brain is normal."

"Figured that was a dead end anyway, but I really enjoyed the Valium," I sighed.

"The DA also wants to meet with you. She's waiting outside and I think she may have an offer," he said tentatively.

I leaned across the table towards him, "What's she got?"

This time, he sighed. "I don't know. Nothing new has come out so I wouldn't expect much."

"Whatever. Bring her in and let's see what she has to say."

Minutes later she entered. Mid- to late thirties, petite, with dark hair, she was more attractive than I remembered. Of course, she transformed back into an evil witch as soon as she opened her mouth.

"Good morning, Mr. Broom. My name is Nora Larson. I am the district attorney dealing with your case. By now you must realize that you have limited options, but we may be willing to make you a deal."

Immediately, my stomach started churning and I clenched my fists under the table.

"Mr. Broom, if you agree to plead guilty to first-degree murder and first-degree attempted murder, we will skip the trial and give you a sentence of sixty years."

Sixty years? Sixty years! There was no way I was going to take sixty years, especially when I never should have been charged with first-degree murder to begin with. Nothing had been premeditated and everyone knew it. So, in my trademark fashion, I made my own offer, "Kiss my ass."

Larson exploded. "Well then, I'll be there when they hook you up to the electric chair, Broom. I look forward to seeing you fry!"

"Yeah, you'll miss me, babe!" I yelled after her as she stormed out of the room.

Silverstein sat in silence, his head hanging down, pretending to shuffle his papers. After a minute of silence, he looked at me and quietly said, "That's not going to help."

"I don't give a shit. I'm sick of screwing around here. I can't take this anymore. Who does she think she is? What about the discrepancy with the date? Can't we use that to get the whole case thrown out?"

"It's all about the timing. We have to wait for the jury to be ready to give the verdict, then they can call a mistrial."

"I can't wait that long. I'm living in the goddamn jungle, Mike. Just use it to get my charges reduced so I can get out on bond. I want a new bond hearing," I demanded.

"You've already been refused twice," Silverstein tried to reason with me.

"Try a third time!" I snapped. That was it. I was going to use the only card up my sleeve so I could get out on bail and take off for Brazil.

Silverstein tried to explain, "If you do that, it will become a tool of the prosecution. They'll just change the date and . . ."

"Just do it!" I pounded my fist on the table.

So Silverstein went to the judge with the motion, and, just as he predicted, bond was refused, the prosecution found out about the date, and the paperwork was fixed before the trial. My one and only get-out-of-jail-free card was played, and I was still facing first-degree murder and first-degree attempted murder charges. Big mouth strikes again.

Chapter Five

AS WINTER SET IN, I FOUND MYSELF WONDERING how the hell I got myself into all this trouble. How did a kid who grew up in the suburbs of upstate New York wind up in a Florida jail awaiting trial for murder? I began to spend my days reflecting on my life, beginning with my earliest memories. Amidst the constant noise and nonsense I escaped into my past each day, trying to recall the twists and turns that led me to this madness.

Oddly, all of my early memories were of me getting into trouble. I didn't remember birthday parties or holidays, just times that I did something wrong or was punished.

One of my first memories was being chased by a goose as a toddler. I was running as fast as a two-year-old could and yelling for help, but the angry goose was in hot pursuit and quickly caught up with me and began pecking at my head. Suddenly my father yanked me behind him, stepping between the giant goose and me. He began swinging and kicking at the bird, but the goose kept fighting back. Finally, after about five minutes, the goose took off down the road, but not without glancing back at me every few steps, as if he was waiting to get another chance at me.

My father, Big Bob, took care of that. He immediately began spanking me, saying, "If you hadn't punched that goose in the beak, he wouldn't have been chasing you down the block, you stupid idiot!" As his powerful arms swung down on me, I kicked my legs up and forward, trying to block him. About ten strikes later, he dragged me into the house. As I thought back about the incident, I realized that I must have been hit before because I already knew how to lessen his blows.

Not too long after this incident, I was sitting on the limb of a tree hammering imaginary nails into it when I found myself looking down at a chained-up German shepherd. Out of sheer curiosity, I leaned over and hit the dog on the head. I wanted to see what he would do. After a loud yelp, he tried to attack me by jumping up on his hind legs, but he couldn't quite reach me. I waited for him to calm down and then did it again and again—laughing wildly all the while. I was having a grand old time until I fell out of the tree; then it was the dog's turn to have some fun. I still have a scar on my cheek where his toenail dug in while he mauled me. Seven stitches later, my parents decided that I was a menace to the neighborhood and myself, and harnessed me to a tree in front of our house.

It didn't take long for me to break free. On the loose, I took off with my friend Jimmy. I was three and a half and Jimmy was only three, so that naturally made me the boss. After skipping stones on the lake that we were supposed to stay away from, we stumbled upon a summerhouse that was closed up for the season. While I wasn't great at skipping stones, I had a great shot for hitting windows, and we promptly broke every window in the house. I remember thinking that it was wrong and reveling in the thrill it.

This led to my first experience with Johnny Law. Later that evening, I found myself locked in a playpen as my mom escorted a state trooper into the house. The tall man with a Smokey-the-Bear type hat slowly leaned over, peered to the bars, and growled at me, "If you ever do that again, you're going to jail, boy. Got me?"

"Uh, yes sir," I croaked, terrified.

My mother shook her head at me and said, "I am so ashamed of you, Dicky."

As the trooper walked out, I heard him say to my mother, "Uh, ma'am, when you first called me, I thought that the offender was a teenager, not a toddler!"

I continued to cause trouble and could always count on retribution. Unfortunately, I wasn't the only one . . . my cat did, as well. One day my father came home and found three claw marks on his prized record cabinet. Furious, he snatched the cat up by the body with one hand and by the back of its head with his other, then snapped its neck. After twitching briefly, he went still. "I hate cats," he growled as he stormed out with Puttie's lifeless body. I quietly cried in the corner, afraid that he might see my tears.

My survival strategy was to escape whenever possible. Luckily, a vast new world opened up to me when we moved to Guilderland. Behind our new house was a gully full of plants and wildlife, including salamanders, squirrels, rabbits, frogs, woodchucks, and muskrats. There were many places to explore in and around the gully and adjoining woods. The nearby brooks trickled into streams, which led to creeks that eventually fed into the Hudson River. No longer harnessed, I was unleashed into the wild and found countless places to play and people to play with.

It was all good until a few months later when school started and I was trapped again. It wasn't long before I started getting into trouble there. From schoolyard fights to pranking the teacher by putting tacks on her chair, I found plenty of ways to get into hot water and often found myself being kept after school.

My teacher, Mrs. Hitchcock, was unusually tolerant of my antics, but one day I pushed her too far and she took me to see the principal, Mr. Z. He was also a fourth-grade teacher and was in the middle of class when she brought me in.

"What's the problem, Mrs. Hitchcock?" he asked.

"Dick Broom!" she said, exasperated.

Mr. Z. went off. "Who do you think you are, Broom? You need to learn some respect. We have rules here and you better get in line, boy!"

After berating me in front of the class, he made me get under his desk to keep me in one place. If I started to squirm, he would kick me. Eventually I settled down and noticed that one of his shoes was untied. Unable to resist, I carefully untied the other shoe and then tied both shoes together. When Mr. Z got up to write on the blackboard he tripped and stumbled to the floor, grasping at his chair to break his fall.

"You rotten kid!" he screamed as I ran from under the desk and out of the school.

I laughed all the way home. I never considered that I might have hurt him; I hadn't really thought things through. I just thought it was funny. That was until I got home. I don't recall the punishment for my hit-and-run on Mr. Z, only the "Jesus Christ!" my dad yelled as he entered the house. The rest was a blur, just a continuation of our battle of wills.

The typical milestones of youth were often overshadowed by my father's undeniable disdain for me. When it was time for me to get my first bicycle, he dragged me to several auctions and garage sales looking for the perfect bike—meaning the cheapest used one he could find. When I asked him why I couldn't get a new bike like all the other kids, he said, "They cost too much and you wouldn't take care of it anyway." After weeks of searching, my mom finally snapped. "Damn it, Bob! Enough already. Get him a new one at Montgomery Wards!" He stormed out of the house without a word, but a few days later a new bike appeared. It was one of the few times I can remember when Mom stood up for me.

I got into many fights at this point. I could always come up with a reason. Most of the time it was to save face in one way or another; for example, I was crappy at basketball, so when other kids would tease me about it, I would come after them. When my parents forced me to take tap-dancing lessons, it was inevitable that the other boys would tease me. I quit the lessons after a while, but not before getting into many brawls over my dancing. I even found a way to get kicked out of the Cub Scouts.

While I got into trouble at home for fighting, on occasion my parents struck a balance and tried not to raise a pushover. In fact, one time a kid three years older than me beat me up and chased me home. When I fled into the house to escape him, my mom spun me around and said, "Don't be such a baby! Get out there and be a man!"

I did. I flew into a rage and beat the older kid to a pulp as my mom watched from the front window.

Violence and anger were simply how our family dealt with conflict. When my mom had a falling-out with her mother, my Nanny, I was told I wasn't allowed to go see her. Nanny was a reliable connection for milk and cookies, however, and she only lived a couple houses away, so I started sneaking over to her house to see her. When my mom got wind of what I was doing, she sent Big Bob after me. He caught me red-handed coming out of Nanny's house and dragged me down the street, screaming and smacking me in the head all the way home, humiliating me in front of the neighbors.

My dad wasn't the only one who hit me. My mom would break out the belt, a paddle, or a switch from time to time. The truth was, in most cases I probably got what I deserved. They only wanted to cause me pain to make me stop doing what I was doing. The problem was that it just didn't work. The worse they got, the worse I got.

Despite the fact that I had a tendency to stir things up, I wasn't all bad—for example, I tried to look out for my classmate John. He was painfully slow at sports and was always the last one picked for any team. I could tell he was trying his best, but he never seemed to get any better. Whenever I had a chance to be team captain, I would select him for my team midway through the process so he wouldn't be the last one standing. I also wouldn't let anyone get away with teasing him in front of me.

This went on for quite some time; then suddenly he stopped showing up at school. I didn't know him that well, so I had no idea what had happened. It wasn't until my mom got a call from John's mother that I found out. John's mom explained that he had passed away from a kidney disease. She called because she wanted to thank me for standing up for John and being his friend. I guess I might have done something right every once in a while.

Still, no matter what I did, it was never good enough. When I ran to help the local fire department fight a fire that was heading toward town, I ended up in trouble with mom for worrying her. After Bob found out that I had an IQ of 138, all he said was that if I was that smart, I should have been doing much better in school.

I could never understand why Big Bob seemed to hate me so much. Mom tried to ignore it, but his utter contempt for me was undeniable. I tried not to let it bother me, and as time went on I think I became numb to it all. It was just easier that way.

Baseball was one of the few things that occasionally brought Big Bob and me together. He taught me how to throw, catch, and hit. He even brought me to New York to see the Yankees play a double-header. In the spring of my fifth-grade year, my principal Mr. Allen approached me about joining his team and Bob gave me the green light.

After learning how to play every position, I discovered a talent for pitching. By the time I hit seventh grade I was a hot shot in the league and was asked to join the all-star team. At midseason we had to go up against a tough team from Albany in a three-game series.

The first game was an away game and when we got there, it was really intimidating. The Albany team had a beautiful field and many of their players seemed a lot bigger than we were. They even had announcers calling the game from a building behind home plate.

"Introducing Scooter, our top player of the season," cheered one of the announcers, as a thirteen-year-old player strutted out to first base. "And now, playing right field, Crazy Legs!"

All of the players' names were announced as they walked onto the field, many of them with slick sounding nicknames. It seemed like we were way out of our league and I could feel my stomach churning.

We were up at bat first and didn't get a single run. It wasn't looking good. It was the first inning and, as the starting pitcher, I nervously walked out to the mound.

"You can do it, Dick! Go Broom!" yelled my grandparents from the bleachers. My whole family was there.

"Don't screw this up, boy!" shouted Big Bob as Mom winced.

Trying to ignore an overwhelming sense of dread, I threw my first pitch. The hitter took a big swing and it was a big miss. Breaking out my curveball, I began striking out player after player. I pitched a three-hit shutout, struck out twelve batters, and got two hits myself. I was the hero for the day, and even Bob didn't have anything bad to say by the end of the game.

The second game of the series was at home and I was called in as a relief pitcher in the sixth inning. We were up 8 to 6, but the bases were loaded and the Albany team had no outs. Again, I was terrified that I would blow the game. Somehow I struck out the next three batters. I remember the third and final out of the game most vividly. It was a one-ball and two-strike count, and I struck out Scooter with my curveball.

The umpire came up to me after the play and smiled. "That was the best curveball we ever saw in Little League!"

By winning the game we won the series, but none of my relatives were at the game. It was probably better that way—no one could burst my bubble.

Fixated on baseball, I started going to watch the high school team play. I had big dreams even though my mom kept telling me I'd never be good enough to make the team. She was proven wrong when I was asked to try out for the ninth-grade team while still in eighth grade. It was a whole different ballpark, with the pitcher's mound now sixty feet from home plate, rather than forty-six. Somehow I made the team.

The following summer I played for the local Kiwanis club and pitched a no-hitter. The beginning of the game was dicey. I ended up walking four guys and they scored a run as a result. After that, the opposing team never even made it to first base, except for one error. Still, Big Bob busted on me after the game for the error, and told me that the only reason it was a no-hitter was because of dumb luck.

I remember being really pissed at him after that. A couple nights later we were outside tossing the ball around and I kept throwing it as hard as I could. He was only wearing a regular glove and my pitch hurt his hand.

"Whoa, kid," he said. "What's wrong with you. You don't want to break my hand do you?"

Without saying a word, I walked back into the house. I don't think he wanted to know the answer.

Chapter Six

DURING THE SUMMER OF MY FOURTEENTH YEAR on this earth, I discovered something that would change my life forever: beer.

On a humid July night, my buddies and I set out on a mission. We liberated a case of beer from the clubhouse at the local golf course and brought it to a nearby park where we were camping out in an elevated platform we built between two trees. Out in the woods, free from any adults, we let loose. Our portable radio blaring Little Richard, we jovially hoisted the beer up into our Tender Trap and immediately began swilling the warm, amber liquid.

"This tastes like shit," I said after my first swill.

"Yeah, it's like panther piss," agreed Robby.

We all paused for a split second, looked at each other, shrugged, and continued to chug it down. About fifteen minutes later a warm glow came over me. It was the best I had felt in my life.

Holding up the can and pointing to it I pronounced, "This is what I've been missing all of my life. Life is good!"

The rest of the guys cheered and pounded the rest of their beers. We continued to drink and after a few more rounds everyone else started to pass out in the jungle hammocks we'd strung up from tree to tree.

My pal Mickey G. and I were the last ones standing—that is, until he tried to piss off the platform and fell off.

"Whoa, brother! You alright down there?" I asked, trying to stifle my laughter.

"Yeah. I'm just gonna crash right here," Mickey slurred before he passed out in a bed of pine needles.

I didn't want the night to end. I was content to sit by myself and finish off the rest of the beers. Listening to the radio, I gazed up through the trees at the beautiful summer sky. It was the first time I ever felt truly free and I wanted to savor the moment. I couldn't believe that it was so easy to feel so good.

By the next morning, I didn't feel so good. I experienced my first official hangover and it wasn't pretty. My stomach was queasy and my head was pounding. Despite it all, I concluded that it was completely worth it and I would pursue that warm fuzzy feeling every chance I got.

The challenge was that my parents were much stricter than the other kids' parents; many times I'd be stuck at home while my friends roamed the neighborhood. Their strategy tended to backfire though because when I did get out, I tried to make up for lost time and have as much fun as possible. Between my growing alcohol consumption and inability to turn down a dare, my adventures usually entailed some form vandalism or hijinx. From blowing up mailboxes with cherry bombs to taking golf balls off the golf course while golfers were still using them, I provided an endless source of entertainment for my friends. I guess you could say I had a bit of wild streak in me.

As my interest in partying went up my grades went down. I had better things to focus on than geometry, like girls and booze. I didn't get to play with either that often, but they were both always on my mind.

My obsession with sports, however, never faltered. By ninth grade, I was playing football, basketball, and baseball, of course. Football was my weakest sport and the only one where I rode the bench. Basketball was a different story. I got much better at it as I got older and, despite the fact that the coach thought I was a delinquent, I played an important role on a winning team.

When it came to baseball, I was golden. As the pitcher for the junior varsity team, I was the main man. We won eight games and lost only one. By the time we took the suburban council junior varsity championship, I was a legend in my own mind. Other people took notice of my talent, too. A coach from the Bethlehem school districts' American Legion team asked me to play for him, even though the league was for sixteen to eighteen year olds and I was only fifteen. The team already had a good pitcher, so I was delegated to relief stints and some starts, but my record was five wins and no losses.

Even Big Bob seemed pleased about it. As a reward, he took me back down to New York to see the Yankees play the Red Sox. It was Ted Williams' last game at Yankee Stadium. During the game, the Yankee's pitcher, Ralph Terry, was on the mound. He threw fastballs and curveballs and kept the ball down around the knees most of the time, but when he didn't, he got hit hard. Around the fourth inning, Dad leaned over to me, smiled, and said, "You throw harder than he does." I couldn't believe it. He thought that at fifteen years old, my fastball was faster than one of the Yankees! I tried to play it cool; I didn't want him to know how much that meant to me. I knew it wouldn't be long till he was disappointed in me again, but I tried to forget that for the afternoon and we actually enjoyed the rest of the day together.

Over the next few years, I also got better and better at basketball. The court was one of the few places where my aggression was considered an asset. Eventually, I got a shot at being a starter and we ended up winning a Christmas tournament in Rensselaer, New York. I made the all-star tournament team, trophy and all. I was also used as a defensive specialist, guarding the top scorer on the other team. Before one game, my buddy Bill broke out a bottle of vodka in the bathroom. This dose of liquid courage made me even more aggressive on the court. I eventually fouled out of the game, but it fed into my reputation of being a wild man—which didn't bother me a bit.

In addition to hanging out with the jocks, I was also running with another rowdy crew that everyone referred to as "the rockers." Most of these friends were older than I was, so they had cars and went to bars. They all wore their hair slicked back and reveled in their reputation for raising hell.

One particularly crazy character I hung out with was Mickey D. He transferred in after living in Chicago. His grandmother who raised him passed away, so he came to live with his only living relative, his uncle who lived in our town. Mickey was hyperactive and always looking for action. He was one of those kids who was too smart for his own good. He had no respect for authority whatsoever and constantly questioned every rule and regulation. When told he didn't need a reason for a rule, he broke it. This made him a perfect fit for our pack of hooligans.

Always the rebel, Mickey used to smoke cigarettes outside a wing of the school. Sometimes he'd ask me to be his lookout and I'd sit inside the door in case some teacher came by. This worked out okay until one day I got impatient waiting for him and went outside to see if he was almost done. Right at that moment, I walked smack into the driver's education instructor who hauled both of us off to see Mr. Carlson, the vice principal.

Back in his office, he questioned me. "Dick, why would you be a lookout for Mickey? He's a troublemaker, a punk."

"He's my friend," I interrupted.

"Friend? He's not your friend. Don't you know that you only have four or five friends in your life and one of them is your mother?"

You don't know my mother, I thought to myself.

"One week detention and I don't want to see you hanging out with that loser again," said Mr. C. "Now get out of my office."

Mickey ended up getting a suspended for that incident and it wasn't long until he was expelled all together. He still hung out with our crew though, serving as our self-appointed social director, coming up with schemes for all sorts of pandemonium. I felt as if he was always there for me. I could always meet his expectations of me because they were never too high. The goals he set were attainable whereas my parents' were not.

Mom and Big Bob hated the kids I was palling around with and wanted me to be spending time with the preppy crowd. They pressed me to join the Key Club because all of the good, up-and-coming citizens were part of it. To appease them, I put my name in the hat, but there were only a dozen students in my grade allowed to join and I wasn't one of them.

When I came home with the news that I didn't make the cut, it didn't go over well. Of course, it was assumed that it was my fault.

"What is wrong with you? What are you, stupid?" cried Mom.

"If you can't get into a club like that you must be as dumb as a rock," grumbled Bob as he left for work.

"Don't you know how important this is? That is where all the best boys are." Mom said, shaking her head.

"I tried, Mom. What do you want from me? They're just a bunch of stuffy assholes anyway," I argued.

She tried to slap me across the face, but this time I stopped her. I was done. I couldn't take it anymore. There was nothing more humiliating. I'd rather be beaten to a pulp by Big Bob than be slapped in the face by her.

From that day on, I never let her slap me again. She tried, but I would block her with my forearm on her forearm and apparently it hurt her. Eventually she gave up and moved on to threatening me: if I didn't let her slap me, she would tell Dad to beat me up when he got home from work. I told her to go ahead and have him come after me, but she was never going to demean me like that again. That was the end of her slapping me, but it certainly wasn't the end of Big Bob's poundings. Now he had an additional excuse for it.

By this point, I just decided that I might as well give them a real reason to come down on me. On Halloween of my junior year, a pack of six or seven of us descended on Altamont to wreak havoc. We knew that the village only had two policemen and two cop cars. But on Halloween night, the two cops decided to ride together and patrol the village in one car. The word on the street was they knew that we were coming.

My brilliant idea was to steal the bubble gum machine off the top of the parked patrol car's roof. What better souvenir of the night than the lights off the top of a police car? Unfortunately, as we were trying with all our might to pull off the lights, the other patrol car came ripping up to us.

"What the hell do you think you're doing," shouted Chief Diehl as he jumped out of the car. There was a reason we called him Big Fucking Deal: he was a giant of a man, six feet seven inches tall and 280 pounds. We all scattered at the sight of him and got away.

Unfortunately, some other kids ratted us out and six days later Big Diehl walked right into my cellar bedroom and confronted me about what happened. After I finally broke down and admitted to the crime, he informed me that he wasn't going to arrest me. "I already talked to your parents and worked out a deal. They are going to handle the sentencing and punishment."

I ended up being grounded for life. No going out after dark. No parties, no dances, no nothing. I guess it would have been worse if they knew that I was stinking drunk that night. They just thought I was stupid or crazy. I could live with that, as long as they didn't take away my buzz.

Being grounded never got in the way of me having a good time. I could still go out during the daytime, so I took full advantage of it. A few months later I went tobogganing with my buddies and a bunch of girls. Going down the small slopes on the local golf course wasn't that thrilling to me until someone broke out a bottle of brandy. It was intended to warm up everyone, but I got hold of it and polished off the bottle within three minutes. Needless to say I was wasted shortly thereafter and became the "big man on the slopes." When no one wanted to go down the hill anymore, I decided to go it alone—which is next to impossible on a toboggan. But with brandy in my blood, I could do anything.

Or so I thought. I took off beautifully but couldn't steer for shit and slammed into a tree stump. After flying into the air, I rammed my left leg, right above the ankle, into the hard, curved wood of the front of the toboggan. In a pathetic attempt to save face, I took a bow and stumbled home.

Luckily, no one was there to bust me for being stinking drunk. I had shooting pains up my leg, but I brushed it off as being a bad bruise. I was on a roll and decided to sneak out to a sock hop. I danced the night away, completely ignoring the pain. The next morning I had a harsh awakening. I couldn't walk at all. My mom drove me to the emergency room and I found out I had a hairline fracture. I had to keep my weight off it for about a month, and then gradually start walking on it until it was completely healed. This was a disaster as it was going to cut into my varsity baseball season. I wouldn't even be able to start training until after the season was already underway.

Without having to work out, I suddenly had a lot more time on my hands to get into trouble. My friend Tony's dad was a contractor working on a new housing development, so we knew how to sneak into the empty houses. A couple times a week we would go there and party. Tony's dad also made wine, so we would drink his "Dago Red" and eat homemade pepperoni, wasting the days away.

I played baseball over the following summer, but also had to go to summer school for math. To make it more bearable, I started stealing the tiny airplane bottles of booze from my parents and smuggling them into school. Mom and Dad had hundreds of the bottles so they never noticed that any were missing. Of course, always the big shot, I made sure the other kids at school noticed what I was up to. Drunk on the bus in the mornings, I would put on a show, singing songs and shaking things up in one way or another. Somehow I also got my hands on a fake ID that said I was twenty-one and got me into even more bars with my rocker crew. We'd ride around in Billy's Buick, blasting Jerry Lee Lewis, Elvis, and any other music that we knew would piss off our parents.

I kept getting into fights all the time: during games, between games, and after games. I was even going with people I didn't know to fight in gang-style rumbles. Fighting made me feel good. It probably had something to do with the fact that I couldn't fight at home. I was forced to live in fear every time Dad came home from work. I was biding my time for the day when I would finally have the balls to knock Big Bob out. In the meantime, I would take on anyone else who gave me shit. No one was going to push me around.

The basketball season ended with our team losing our last four games, which knocked us out of the regional playoffs because of a third place finish in the league. When we lost the last game of the season, I was full of rage but had no one to hit. I ended up breaking down and crying in front of some drinking buddies, which only made me feel worse. I was ashamed for not winning and even more so for showing emotion.

I tried to pull myself together and make up for the disappointment by focusing on the upcoming baseball season. When our other pitcher hurt his arm, the bulk of the pitching was left up to me. It was a lot of pressure, but I did well and pitched a no-hitter about halfway through the season, making Dad proud.

But that was a fleeting moment. I ended up being suspended from school immediately after the game because of something that had happened a few days prior to the game. Earlier that week I was on my way to lunch when my compadre Russell pulled out a firecracker and said, "I bet you wouldn't fire this off in the cafeteria."

Unable to resist, I grabbed the firework and responded, "Give me a match!"

Minutes later everyone was screaming and fleeing the cafeteria, thinking that a bomb had gone off. I got away with it at first. It took forty-four hours until the school administrators brought me in after someone ratted me out. I thought of it as an innocent prank, but apparently I had a gift for timing. There happened to be a group of foreign exchange students visiting in the cafeteria at the time the fireworks went off, and somehow the explosion was misconstrued as an assassination attempt. The feds came in to investigate and the school had to tell them, "No, it was just this asshole Dick Broom throwing a firecracker."

Interestingly, they waited until after I pitched that no-hitter to suspend me.

The season ended with a three-way tie for first place with me losing after pitching a one-hitter—an infield single at that. We lost the game 1 to 0.

Somehow, despite all my bullshit, I ended up getting accepted into three colleges. Of course, Dad was furious because I just missed getting into the Coast Guard Academy by a tenth of a percentage point. I had done well on the tests to get in, scoring a 98 in science, 94 in math, and 89 in English. What brought me down was the 74 on the psychological test. Imagine that.

Chapter Seven

AFTER GETTING TWO BLACK EYES AT MY PROM, I graduated high school and tried to enjoy my last summer before I was off to college. I got a job microfilming records at the New York State Department of Banking. While I was a hard worker, I wasn't one to shy away from indulging in some liquid lunches with the rest of my coworkers. My boss was also my American Legion baseball coach, so he never gave me a hard time. He'd yell at the older guys in the office for tossing down a bunch of beers and coming back an hour late, but he always let me slide.

The main reason for this was that I was one of his best players. In fact, one of the wins for his team that season was probably the greatest game I ever pitched. We were up against a team of all-star players from various Catholic schools in the area, a bunch of who were already playing college ball. I pitched a no-hitter, striking out fifteen batters and walking one. At the end of the game, everyone on my team spontaneously rushed the mound to congratulate me, even my coach.

As I strutted off the field, head held high, Big Bob's first words were, "How come you walked that one batter?" Immediately my shoulders hunched over. When the umpire came up to tell me that it was the best-pitched game he had ever witnessed, I still felt defeated, even though we had won the game.

Two and half weeks later, we were up against the same team. I was the starting pitcher, except this time I was still drunk from the night before. With my buzz still on, I didn't give a shit about the game. After three innings, the coach pulled me off the mound and I went behind a nearby building for a smoke. As I lit up, a well-dressed guy approached me.

"Hey, Broom. What's wrong with you today?" he asked. Before I could give him a smart answer, he leaned over and got a whiff of me. "Punk kid," he muttered to himself as he shook his head and walked away. I found out later that he was a scout for Philadelphia. Many scouts were showing up to see me play in those days, but they seemed to stop coming around after that.

Although the scouts didn't come around, the girls sure did. One of the greatest perks of playing sports is the attention you get from the ladies. I ended up spending that summer dating one girl, Toni, who chased me down after reading about me in the paper. She was an actress and definitely had a flair for being dramatic. She put on quite a show, convincing me that she was in love with me. I fell for it until I found out that she also had a couple of other boyfriends. It was actually a relief to me, as we broke up right before I left for college. That meant I was going to be free to play the field once I got there. I'd picked Cortland State because there were three girls to every guy and I was looking forward to having a good time.

I wouldn't say that I was a playboy—more of a freelancer. I liked to have a girlfriend, but also wanted to play the field without any consequences. There were plenty of beautiful girls at Cortland, and once I joined the basketball team it didn't take any effort to get a date. The problem was, there was nowhere to go for some action. We couldn't go to the dorms, so the only two options left were the woods and the cemetery. For some reason, both places were a hard sell. When I finally lost my virginity, it was with a big fat townie who was doing it with everyone. Technically, I wasn't even a virgin when I was with her. I had already slept with a hooker in Albany. It wasn't the only time I was with a hooker, but it was the only time I had to pay for it. By the time I got to jail I must have been with over 500 women and was in just as many fights.

Between chasing skirts and parties, it didn't take me long to get behind on my schoolwork. Without Mom and Big Bob around to bust my chops, I did a lot of procrastinating. It didn't hurt that I easily found a bunch of other guys who had the same gift for getting nothing done. Most of them came from New York City, including my roommate, Brian. He was nineteen and had already been asked to leave two other colleges. My mom knew right away that he was going to be a bad influence on me. She met him the day she and Dad dropped me off at school and immediately pulled me aside to say, "I want you to move!" Maybe it was because he started rambling on about his correspondence with Fidel Castro. Mom shouldn't have worried about him skewing my political views. I didn't give a shit about politics. I just wanted to party.

Free from the wrath of Big Bob, I vowed that no one would ever tell me what to do again. As a result, I didn't respond well to the freshman hazing. I refused to wear the stupid beanie and told the upperclassmen that I wasn't playing along with that silly shit. They tried to pressure me into it by calling me a bad sport, but they gave up quickly once they realized what a pain in the ass I was determined to be.

Just a few weeks into the semester, I was raising hell and making a lot of noise outside one of the dorms in the middle of the night. A couple of older guys, probably around twenty-five-years old, came out to quiet me down.

One of them was a monster; he was about six feet two inches tall and 230 pounds, with a buzz cut. "Okay, chump. Time to go back to your dorm and pass out," he said calmly.

"Fuck off! I don't have a curfew," I challenged as I stormed up to him.

We were nose to nose, and he didn't blink. "Go back to your room, now!"

"Fuck you!" I said, trying not to blink either.

"Listen, asshole. I'm the dean of men and I'm telling you that you will regret this. It's only a matter of time until I bust you again for another violation and you can bet that I'll remember this."

After taking a moment to register what he was saying, I turned around and staggered back to my dorm.

Much of my time at Cortland was spent drunk. There was always someone partying somewhere who could appreciate my company. Sometimes I sought them out; sometimes they suckered me in. One Saturday, for example, I was coaxed by my punk friends to go to an afternoon dance. While I intended to just dance, I broke down when I got there and discovered they were having beer-chugging contests. Naturally, my competitive nature forced me to join in. After winning a couple rounds, I finally lost a round and was out of the running. But I kept on drinking for the rest of the party.

That would have been fine except I had a basketball game that night. I tried to straighten up before the game by going back to my dorm room to clean myself up. While gargling Listerine to cover up the alcohol on my breath, the thought crossed my mind that should I belch during the game, the beer smell would come wafting up. To prevent this from happening, I came up with the ingenious idea to drink the whole bottle; then I showed up at the game an hour later.

The coach didn't seem to notice a thing and, as I was warming up, an amazing thing happened: I began dunking the ball easily. Previously, I could only dunk once in a while during lay-up drills, but this night I was jumping eight or ten inches higher and could easily dunk with two hands. After realizing this, I put on quite a show. I played wicked defense, holding the opposing team's top scorer to three points, blocking at least three of his jump shots, scoring underneath with offensive rebounds, and being a terror until I fouled out with six minutes left in the game. The only drawback was that three minutes later I had to run back to the locker room to puke for about fifteen solid minutes. Aside from that, it was probably my best game of the season, and I concluded that there were many things I could do better while drunk: dance, fight, *and* play basketball.

It wasn't long after that I was declared academically ineligible to play basketball. It came as no surprise to me. All I did was screw around. I never spent any time on academics. When was I supposed to study? I was too busy wrestling, singing doo-wop, and having fart-lighting contests! Rather than buckling down and becoming motivated to work harder, I just partied even more. I started hitting the bars in town during the week and stealing money to pay for my drinking.

Everything came to a head in March when I got into a brawl in a downtown bar called the Tavern. I was so drunk I don't even remember how the fight started, all I can recall is kicking the hell out of two older guys sitting in a booth, until one of them broke a beer mug over my head. It split my skull open, and I walked to the hospital holding some bar towels on my head to soak up the blood.

The next day I got some clarification on what happened from the dean of men—the same one I had told to fuck off a couple months earlier.

"Mr. Broom, the two gentleman that you attacked last night are employed by the college as assistant professors. As I told you months ago, it would only be a matter of time until we met again. This time, I'm not going to ask you to go back to your dorm. I'm telling you that you are going home. You are immediately suspended from Cortland State for a semester and a half. Call your parents and have them pick you up."

I wasn't sure what was fueling my pounding head: my hangover, head wound, or the thought of calling home. "You dumb piece of shit," were the first words out of Big Bob's mouth, and it went downhill from there.

The three-hour ride home was, in a word, humiliating. The first half hour consisted of Mom telling me how embarrassed she was and Bob ranting and raving about how I was going to get a goddamn job and tow the line, or else. Of course, he didn't need to explain what "or else" meant, but he did, in graphic detail. The rest of the trip was spent primarily in silence, with each of them occasionally reiterating their disappointments and threats. When we finally got home, I snuck down into the cellar and hid.

The tension around the house was palpable, so I set out to get a job right away so I could escape the house and get Bob off my back. It wasn't long before I was hired as an orderly at Albany Medical Center, where a number of the elderly patients mistook me for a doctor. Within two weeks after being hired, though, I lost my job after dislocating my shoulder playing basketball.

I spent a couple of weeks recovering and was unable to do anything, which infuriated Bob. Even my mom acted put-upon. It was no picnic for me either. I was stuck at home most of the time, trying to keep a low profile in order to avoid dealing with their wrath.

One afternoon I was quietly walking down the hall and heard my mom talking on the phone. I didn't intend to eavesdrop, but stopped dead in my tracks when I heard her say, "I don't know what to do. He's acting just like his real father. He was a drunk, too."

Who the hell was she talking about? My entire body started to tremble as I stood in silence outside the kitchen door.

"The whole reason why he got kicked out of college was because of his drinking. He's completely out of control. His father was the same way. That's why I left him. I don't know what to do. Bob is losing his patience. He's put up with a lot considering he's not even his real son."

At that, I ran out of the house and down the street. My mind was spinning. I couldn't believe what I heard. If Bob wasn't my real father, who the hell was? I knew Bob had hated me for all these years, and now I knew why. Flashes of his abuse raced through my head. He never should have done that as my dad. It was even worse that he wasn't my real father! I vowed to myself that the next time he tried to come near me, I would bust him up.

After walking aimlessly around the neighborhood for a couple hours, I slipped into the house and went back down into the cellar. I didn't let Mom know what I heard and kept to myself over the next few days. When I finally was alone at home, I sat down at my mom's desk and opened up a drawer where I knew she kept her important papers. There, among her files, was my birth certificate. It listed my name as Richard Brion Tremper, son of Gloria and Charles Tremper. Behind that paper in the file was another document certifying my adoption by Big Bob.

It was official. I was the flesh and blood of some guy named Charles, not Bob. No wonder I always got the brunt of Big Bob's frustration. It only took a moment for my self-pity to turn to rage. All my life I was treated like a burden to everyone. I was my mother's cross to bear, and Bob's "child" to put up with—if he wanted to be with Mom.

I quickly put the papers away and went to see my friend Ray. He knew something was wrong as soon as he saw my face.

"You won't believe this shit!" I choked up, trying not to break down. As I told him what happened, he didn't seem that surprised and neither did his mom. I realized that she went to high school with my mom, so she may have already known. Ray's reaction was telling as well, but I didn't have it in me to ask him if he knew about it, too. He was a good friend and probably didn't know how to bring it up with me. He sat and listened to me and helped me calm down so I could go home.

I decided not to say anything to anyone about what I knew until the time was right. It didn't take long for that moment to arise. Just a few days later, I pissed Bob off and he came at me. This time I didn't take it and knocked him on his ass. In a fury, I started pounding on his head, screaming at him, "Who the hell do you think you are? I'm not even your son, you bastard." Stunned, he stopped fighting back and I stood up. Without a word, he went to the bedroom and shut the door.

Not a word was said about it over the next week. One afternoon I came back drunk from playing cards with some of my old high school chums. Big Bob was standing in the driveway as I stumbled out of my buddy's car.

"You goddamn drunk!" he exclaimed. "It's the middle of the afternoon, for Christ's sake! You are nothing but a worthless piece of shit! You better get a job, boy, and don't even think you're going out tonight."

"Fuck off, asshole. You can't tell me what to do. You're not my father," I said as I brushed passed him on my way to the front door.

Infuriated, Bob grabbed a baseball bat from just inside the garage door. "If you try to go out, I'll knock your pea-brained head off!"

"Bring it on!" I said and charged him.

He smacked me in the left temple, but not hard enough. I grabbed the bat out of his hand, took a swing at him, and knocked him onto the front lawn. "This is for the time you dragged me down the street from my grandmother's house!" I shouted as I used all my might to slam him with the bat. I continued to beat him as I recalled the countless times he had done the same to me. This went on until two state troopers showed up and pried the bat away from me. Apparently my neighbors called them because they thought I was trying to kill him. Maybe I was.

For some reason, the cops believed me when I told them that I was just defending myself. I was obviously as emotional as hell and they tried to calm me down. "Okay, son, we hear you. Just get out of here before we have to arrest you. Go stay somewhere else tonight."

Taking their advice, I caught up with one of my baseball buddies, Matt, who had just gotten into a fight with his old man as well. I guess "Father Knows Best" didn't quite ring true in a number homes in our neighborhood.

Matt and I headed into town to find some girls. While standing on the corner talking to a group of ladies, some guy, not knowing what he was stepping into, walked by and made a smart-ass remark.

"What the fuck did you say?" I asked.

Before the guy could answer, I let out the rest of my rage on him. After I broke his nose, Matt and I continued our binge and ended up passing out at a nearby motel.

It wasn't long before I heard that there was an arrest warrant put out on me for assault. Two days later I turned myself in to Judge Bixby. He knew me most of my life as I used to be his paperboy, and he let me off with six months probation. If I could stay out of trouble for that period, the record would be expunged.

I knew there was no way I could stay out of trouble if I went back home, so I moved in with my Nanny and tried to pull myself back together. While she wasn't happy about what happened with Bob, she understood why it happened and took the opportunity to fill me in about my real dad. I didn't ask her about him, but she kept telling me stories about him anyway.

Apparently, he was a musician and an alcoholic. Mom started dating him while Bob was fighting the war and she ended up getting pregnant. No matter what he did, he was never able to sober up. He tried though. He even walked ninety miles to Poughkeepsie to a mental institution to get "the cure," but slipped back into drinking. His relationship with Mom fell apart soon after. When Bob returned from the war, he was devastated to find out his high school sweetheart had a child with another man. Somehow, he forgave her . . . but he never forgave me.

Chapter Eight

NANNY CONTINUED TO FILL ME IN WITH TALES about Charles that I didn't want to hear. To escape her stories, I signed up for a couple classes at a community college and picked up a night job working at the local Coke plant. I spent over sixty backbreaking hours a week loading trucks and kept missing classes because I was always too tired to go to school. I made enough money to buy a new car and found time to play baseball over the summer, but I was miserable at work and knew that I needed a change.

As luck would have it, I ran into my old pal Johnny who told me the federal government was paying tuition for students to become techs for their new nuclear power plants. I jumped at the chance and enrolled in the program at Hudson Valley Community College right away. I never formally quit my job at the Coke plant; I just blew them off to go to a party one night and never came back.

School ended up being very demanding. Suddenly, I had an enormous course load. I was signed up for eighteen credit hours, but when you counted the labs, it added up to about twenty-four hours

of classes a week. Chemistry, calculus, physics, physiology, and eco-
nomics . . . it wasn't long before I realized that some of the classes
were beyond my comprehension.

As usual, school didn't get in the way of my having a good time.
When I found out that the girl-to-guy ratio was the opposite of
Cortland, and the frat boys were the only ones who got the ladies
there, I decided I could swallow my pride and handle a little bit of
hazing in order to get laid. So, after playing baseball that fall, I
pledged a fraternity. For eleven and a half weeks I was humiliated in
the cafeteria, called out to the frat house at night to do push-ups and
squats against the wall, and endured all the other standard pledging
fare. The final two weeks were the worst, culminating with twenty-
four hours of torture. It was an emotionally and physically demanding journey, but somehow it all seemed worth it. Not only did it give
me a strong sense of accomplishment, it also got me into a frat
house where there were countless parties and plenty of chicks.

Classes quickly became an afterthought, but I did work hard
when I got a job at a local bar called the Timber. The Timber Inn was
a family-run business, headed up by the widowed matriarch of the
family, Kathy. She was a tough old bird who had had two husbands
drink themselves to death. She was never wrong, and every day she
would show me a different way to mop the floor, pour a beer, or
make a sandwich. She had three sons, and they would all want me to
do things differently as well. The four of them were constantly at
each other's throats and thought nothing of arguing with one
another in front of their customers. At my age and with my attitude,
I thrived on their chaos.

There's no doubt that I learned more working there than I ever
did in college. I dealt with many customers with all types of jobs,
from all walks of life. I'd be pouring beers for college kids, whiskey
for construction workers, and pink ladies for local television person-
alities. In addition to the bar, we had a banquet room where we

could cater parties for up to sixty people and an outside pavilion where we would host clam bakes and steak roasts from late spring through early fall. I did everything there: cooking, waiting tables, bartending—whatever they needed, whenever they needed it. The job was a perfect fit for my lifestyle. I drank as much as I wanted to, then as much as I could handle . . . and, finally, enough to get me through the day.

By Christmas I had moved into the frat house and was drinking everyday. A big man on campus, I was hanging out with the coolest guys within our fraternity—Josh, Rup, George, and Crackers. The Beatles had just come to America, so we all grew our hair long and gained the reputation for being party boys. We would start off every Saturday with either a big bowl of punch made mostly of liquor, or a freshly tapped keg, then invite some local high school girls over to watch cartoons and play. After our morning romps with the teenie boppers, we would rest up for a frat party or a trip into downtown Troy later that night.

By this point, I knew that radiological biology and public health were not for me. I was bombing in my classes, but I hung onto the major because it allowed me to go to college for free. I didn't care about learning anything. I just wanted to continue living my life as a carefree frat boy.

Despite my failing grades, some of my frat brothers thought that I still knew more than they did. When George was failing his general science class, for example, he asked me to take the midterm for him. Since I was taking all of these advanced courses, and he had an average of 40 in the class, I guess he thought that I couldn't possibly do any worse.

I agreed to take the test and it was a cakewalk. Everything on it was crap I covered in eighth grade. He got a 98 on the test, but his professor knew something was up—not only because he had suddenly done so well on the test, but because I had misspelled his name. I wrote "Gorge" instead of George. He ended up being kicked out for a semester because of it.

I thought I finally got my big break when I was invited to try out with the Kansas City Athletics baseball team. I wasn't in the best shape because of all my partying, but my arm was in fair condition. A couple of weeks before the tryout my own college coach was asked to take over the semi-pro Kansas City team. I didn't really like the coach because he treated me like I was his "project" and was constantly busting my balls. The night before the tryout he had me pitch against a good team. He kept pressuring me to throw curve balls and I did, not because he was my coach, but because he had the power to get me onto the Kansas City team. I ended up pitching a one-hit shutout and we won the game.

The next day, I woke up to find that my forearm near my elbow was all swollen. Naturally, this blew my tryout because I couldn't even throw the ball ten feet. I spent the afternoon trying to tell the Kansas City scouts about the great game I played the night before, but none of them would give me the time of day.

Later that night I realized that my coach knew that curve balls strain the elbow, and I concluded that he must have sabotaged me on purpose. I knew he was sick of my attitude and wanted to show me who was the boss. I decided to show him that he couldn't control me: I quit the team and never pitched at Hudson Valley again.

The next school year was a blur. There were plenty of frat parties, plenty of girls, and certainly plenty of fights: mostly bar room brawls, some parking lot battles, a few in fields, a couple in alleys, and a handful down by the Hudson River.

One night I hooked up with some of my old high school buddies to go to the opening of a quasi-arcade way out in the country. It was a family business owned by a guy, Anthony, that I went to college with. The place was cool; it had pinball machines, pool tables, and a couple of wooden bowling alleys. Of course, the real reason we were there was because they were giving away free beer. As soon as we got there, we started pounding beers, and my old baseball buddy, Gary, drank as much as he could within a half-hour's time.

"Hey, Broom, check this out!" he shouted as he tossed one of the bowling balls overhand at the pins.

"You need more practice, brother," I laughed. "It's not a baseball. You've got to work on your aim."

After Gary tossed three more balls, Anthony's father growled, "That's enough. Give me the ball."

Drunk as a skunk, Gary wouldn't hand it over. He threw it at one of the pinball machines instead.

"Okay wise guy, no more beer for you or any of your friends!"

That was when I knew I had to get involved. I went behind the bar and started to pour a beer. Anthony's brother came up and tried to turn off the tap. At that, I snapped. I grabbed an empty coffee percolator and smashed it over his head. Another brother came at me and I knocked him out, and subsequently did the same to both Anthony and his father. As I was walking out the door, I threw his fifteen-year-old brother through the front window. All of this happened in under two minutes and before we were even out of the parking lot, we were all back to being our jovial selves. It was as if a switch was turned on and then off.

While we barely gave the incident a second thought, Anthony's family did. The next time I saw him he told me that I would either pay for the damages or his family would have me arrested since I was the only one he knew. I called the guys who were with me that night and they pitched in to cover the price of the extortion. Looking back, I knew what I did was wrong, but the only reason I cared then was because it cost me money.

My temper ended up hitting me in the wallet again just a few months later. Our fraternity was invited by a brother fraternity to a party on their campus at Rensselaer Polytechnic Institute (called

RPI). A bunch of our brothers went, bringing dates from a sorority at our college. Our dates were the only girls there, and the guys from the other frat started hitting on them within ten minutes of our arrival. We decided to leave and as we were getting our coats, some of the RPI brothers tried to stop us. One of them was a hockey player who thought he was a badass. Of course, I thought I was one too, so this encounter turned out to be a problem. I solved it quickly by knocking out a couple of his front teeth. In the heat of the fight, one of his brothers hit me on the head with the edge of a beer can, opening up a gash behind my left ear. The night added up to me getting five stitches and having to pay for the hockey player's dental bill.

There was no denying that my rage at the world and most of the people in it began costing me pain and money. Of course, alcohol seemed to play a consistent role as well. I didn't get into trouble every time I drank, but every time I got into trouble I was drinking.

Chapter Nine

IN THE SPRING OF 1966, FEDERAL LAWS CHANGED AND suddenly, being in college no longer shielded you from the draft. The war was building up and the Pentagon needed bodies, so they decided to require male college students to take a test to prove they were actually learning something in college. The exam was like an aptitude test and I always did well on them, so I wasn't worried.

The day of the test there was a water main break and the administration cancelled all classes for the rest of the day. The test was scheduled for 3:00 PM. At 9:00 AM I was in the Timber bar with over a hundred other students enjoying some cocktails. We decided to seize the day and took three kegs and a case of wine up to Thatcher Park in the nearby Heidelberg Mountains, about fifteen miles from campus.

My game plan was to party until about 1:30 and then head over to the test. But when it came time to leave, I was involved in some important conversations and even more important drinking. Rather than taking off, I uttered those two magic words that I would often say for the next sixteen years: "Fuck it."

About two months later I received an "invitation" to join the army on October 7. I had to take a physical the week before and despite my sports injuries, like a recurring dislocated shoulder, the draft board still found me fit for duty. They must have been desperate. By this point I was boozing it up every day, so I was overweight and out of shape. I guess they would take anyone they could get, even me.

On October 6, I got myself ready to head out by hitting the bars with my high school chums, Ray, Mickey, and Eddie. After having a couple cocktails at one place, my friends convinced me to go into Marvin's Pub for one last drink, even though I was banned from there for some foolish behavior a year ago. When we got there, Marvin wasn't out front and the bartender didn't know me, so I had no problem getting served. I was disappointed because I was hoping Marvin would refuse to let me in, and then I could tell him exactly what I thought of him.

As if someone up above heard my wish, Marvin magically appeared from the kitchen as I was drinking my beer.

"Get the hell out of here!" he yelled as he reached for my beer.

"C'mon, Marvin. Give me a break," I said, half-jokingly. "I'm going into the army tomorrow to help secure free enterprise, ergo your business . . ."

"Cut the shit, Broom. I want you out right now!" With that he picked up a full bottle and threatened me with it.

I promptly responded by knocking him on his ass with a left foot to his balls and a right cross to his noggin. The bartender jumped in and I knocked him out with a single punch to the jaw. Next came a foolish patron who soon landed on his ass, as well. I bolted out, jumped in Mickey's car, and we drove ten miles to a rock club out in the country.

Within an hour, the state troopers came in looking for me. I slipped out the back to hide, but after a couple of minutes, my curiosity got the best of me and I peeked back inside to see what was going on. I was spotted immediately and arrested. "I guess I'll be no good doing reconnaissance in the army!" I joked to my boys as the cops escorted me out of the bar.

Big Bob showed up to bail me out. We had spoken only a few times since our blowout, but I was staying at their house for the few days leading up to my induction. On October 9, I was brought before the judge. He gave me a choice between prison and the army. After a moment's thought, I gave my answer and the judge dropped the charges.

The next morning, October 10, I reported for duty. I was three days late due to my incarceration, and the officer in charge immediately gave me shit for going AWOL before even swearing in. Apparently he knew what happened because when we arrived in Albany for our flight down to the base in Columbia, South Carolina, he got right into my face and said, "You like to fight, Broom? Here," and he shoved the personnel files for all the guys on the flight into my arms. "Anybody tries to take these from you, fight for them." I held on to the records for the flight and for the train ride out to Fort Jackson. Once there, I was relieved of the duty.

The first few days there were a blur. We took hours of tests to see where our strengths were as well as our intellectual weaknesses. When we weren't taking tests we were being measured for our uniforms and getting shots. After a couple days, I found out that I had scored very high on the math and IQ tests and was sent out to Fort Carson, Colorado, for artillery-based training.

So far, the army sucked. It was only three years ago when I swore to myself that no one would ever tell me what to do again. Now I was being ordered to make my bed, shine my shoes, fold my clothes a certain way, eat fast, run everywhere I went, and march. Most of the time I was too exhausted to argue, but when I did it just made everything suck even more.

Within four weeks we were finally able to get out to the firing range, sight in our M14 rifles, and eventually fire at targets. I was looking forward to this and quickly learned how to shoot properly. Eventually I earned a sharpshooter medal that I could wear on my dress greens.

Not surprisingly, I also did well in the fighting pits. There we would get to fight other soldiers in sand pits with plastic replicas of rifles with bayonets (called pugle sticks). After winning the battery championship and the battalion championship, I ended up beating the best guys from another battalion, two at a time. They even brought in a general and colonel to watch me fight that day; it was the first time I felt real pride in a long time.

Once basic training was over, I went on leave for a week and went back to Albany. I made the most of my time there, getting laid and into a couple of fights. Then it was off to what they call Advanced Individual Training or AIT. My high math scores led to me being placed in Fire Direction Control Training—or what the Army referred to as the brains of the artillery. This was ten weeks of learning how to hit a target up to eighteen miles away. The training consisted of classroom time and live fire in the field.

To liven things up, I would get weekend passes to take off for Colorado Springs. The challenge was that I only made $90 a month and that was never enough to cover my drinking when I went out. I quickly figured out that in terms of getting a buzz on, buying a half-gallon of cheap wine and drinking it on my way into town was a cheaper way to go.

One of my best getaways while out west was a long weekend in Aspen. Several of my college pals were working as bartenders and living at some of the ski lodges there. I hitched up Interstate 25 from Colorado Springs to Denver and then caught a Greyhound the rest of the way. I was a little nervous heading out onto the road by myself, but was excited to get away from the army. I had a four-day pass due to Lincoln's and Washington's birthdays and I was ready to make the most of it.

My college buddies Donnie Mac and Ron picked me up at the bus station, along with a young lady from Sweden who was apparently mine for the taking if I wanted her. Back at their chalet, I took advantage of the Swiss Miss and spent the next few days in a whirlwind of drinking and sex. My friends knew a guy who would scam the liquor store for booze, so I was drinking for free the entire time I was there.

Sometime during this particular bender, I got tired of Swiss Miss and met an all-American cutie who went to college in Boulder. We hit it off famously, especially in bed, and made plans for me to visit her in Boulder sometime in the near future. Somehow, four days turned into five, and I returned to duty a day late. Luckily, my drunken platoon sergeant was also AWOL and during the confusion of his absence, mine was overlooked.

A couple of weeks later I hooked up with my newfound honey in Boulder. After some much-needed sex, I began drinking wine and helping her get ready for a little dinner party she had planned for the evening. The menu consisted of tacos, which I had never had before. By the time her friends came, I had put down two bottles of wine and was toasted. Trying to be funny, I started a taco fight. I began hurling tacos onto her walls and the refrigerator, making a giant mess. She didn't think it was at all funny.

"What is wrong with you? Are you crazy?" she yelled as she tried to get the tacos away from me.

I still thought it was funny and continued to toss salsa onto the ceiling.

"Get the hell out of here, you insane asshole. Right now or else I'm calling the cops!" she threatened.

At that, I fumbled around to get my stuff and staggered out of her apartment. It wasn't the last time I would act like a childish asshole and screw up a good thing. As time went on, I became an expert at it.

Soon after the taco incident, I was put on permanent duty in an 8-inch Howitzer group to await my orders to ship out to Vietnam. Fortunately, these orders never came and I spent the rest of my time in Colorado Springs, waking up each morning to a view of Cheyenne Mountain. I even played on the Fort Carson baseball team and traveled all over the West playing college teams. Sometime the team would travel for a week or more, which was a welcome escape from the boring army grind. I also coached a little league basketball team in the winter.

On Christmas leave, I journeyed back home to New York and met a girl who would end up being my first wife and first divorce. Let's call her Wilma because she probably hates my guts now. She was a hot brunette with a killer body and dimples. We began a whirlwind romance and within a few months she came out to Colorado to play house. I somehow found myself at the El Paso County Courthouse getting married that May.

We got off to a rocky start. For some reason, she didn't appreciate the fact that I pitched a baseball game on our wedding night. I had to do it; if I didn't, I would have been considered AWOL. Although Wilma said she understood, she kept bringing it up for years to come. What really sucked was that we didn't even win the game.

Marriage didn't exactly settle me down. I still got into tons of fights and continued to party. By this point, I had found new ways to get high. Who knew there were so many options? Pot, hash, LSD, barbiturates, Librium—I indulged in all of them. I even injected methamphetamines several times. My drinking slowed down a bit, but I still found creative ways to consume alcohol. For example, I discovered that if I poured half a gallon of cheap wine like Paisano or Wild Irish Rose into a bong, I could get really wasted. I would smoke some hash or pot through it first and then drink the now bitter-tasting wine. For some reason, I thought this magic potion turned me into a super lover. I doubt that Wilma agreed.

Along with the drugs came the concerts. We saw Van Morrison, Cream, and Jefferson Airplane at the Family Dog in Denver. We also caught Jimi Hendrix and Vanilla Fudge at Red Rocks Amphitheatre. With my military buzz cut, I was taken for a cop by many of the longhairs there. Of course, the truth is that some of the longhairs were the real narks. I was as high as the Rockies for the shows and, even so, often got bored. I never really enjoyed the psychedelic, groovy crap. I'd much rather be drinking in a bar than staring at the walls trying to look cool.

On the morning of October 9, 1968, I received my discharge papers. It was the official end of my army career. I was elated: no more standing at attention at 7:00 AM every morning, and no more being told what to do by some lifer idiot. While I did learn some things in the army, like time management and a bit more patience, I was grateful to get out, especially without having to go to Vietnam. Many guys I knew died over there or were seriously injured. I was lucky. Not only did I avoid that hellhole, but I was also eligible for a disability check and free medical coverage because of an injury to my shoulder that happened during maneuvers in the field. The injury required me to have an operation that left a giant scar on my left shoulder, but with intensive therapy I recovered completely. For this, I would get the same care as the poor guys who fought in the jungle and came home without arms and legs. I couldn't help but feel a bit guilty about it.

Chapter Ten

WHEN THE BIG DISCHARGE DAY CAME, WE PILED everything into my 1957 Chevy and headed back to the East Coast with a new sense of optimism. As I drove cross-country with my new wife by my side, I looked forward to starting a new job with the ironworkers' union, where I would finally be making good money When our car broke down outside of Pittsburgh I should have taken that as a sign of what was to come, but I clung to the hope that things were finally going to come together.

After being picked up by Wilma's brother, we made it up to Albany where I started working on the new legislative building downtown. Everything was going smoothly until another worker came back to the construction site from lunch drunk and almost knocked me off the fifth floor. Suddenly, I became terrified of heights and had to leave the job because I couldn't bring myself to go up there again.

As usual, when all else failed, I turned to alcohol. In this case, I picked up a job working as a bartender at a thousand-seat restaurant called Wally's Steak House. The money was less than half of what I was making with the union, but I worked overtime and also picked up another gig working as a bouncer at a nightclub. I wasn't exactly the ideal husband, and that's putting it mildly. Once I had a few cocktails in me, I pretty much forgot that I was married, and with late shifts, free drinks, and countless cocktail waitresses, I often didn't come home until five in the morning.

Things started to change when we found out that Wilma was pregnant. Wilma's dad, Bill, was loaded, and once the news broke about the baby, we moved out of our cool apartment in Schenectady into a house on his horse farm out in the sticks. This worked out great for everyone except me, since I was still working so far away. I eventually broke down and quit my job to go work with Bill at the nearby country club.

On July 11, 1969, my daughter Kathryn Ann was born. I fell in love with Katie at first sight. I finally had someone to play with who was my age emotionally. We had a lot in common. Both of us would sob or throw a tantrum when we didn't get our way.

Although I adored my daughter, her birth didn't slow me down at all. Two months later returned to college at Hudson Valley, but as a liberal arts student this time. I went back to working at Wally's because I was laid off from the country club for the season. I don't know how I did it, going to school and working full-time. I was still getting drunk every night at work, but I somehow found a way to juggle it all. The army taught me how to manage my time, so I never wasted a minute. Whenever I had an open period during the day, I would find an empty classroom to do my schoolwork and ended the semester on the dean's list with a 3.3 average.

I took pride in doing well as a student and did everything I could to keep up. I knew that hard work had its rewards. I may have been many things, but I was never lazy. Wilma, on the other hand, never seemed to do shit. She hadn't worked since we got back from Colorado and didn't lift a finger around the house. While I was going nonstop from classes to work, she couldn't even do the dishes.

She was used to being a spoiled princess, and I had no problem telling her so. Of course, this led to a number of fights. Most of them were just verbal, but she did break a lamp over my head at one point. Naturally, the story was twisted around and all everyone else heard was that I hurt her shoulder. I never got physical with her. I may have been a philandering, nasty drunk, but I saved my brawling for the general public.

By this point, I was getting into fights even when I didn't want to. My fraternity brothers had a penchant for starting trouble and often counted on me to finish it. One Sunday night I was sobering up for the drive home to my wife and child, when a call came in for back-ups. A seedy guy named Benny, who was our frat's pot dealer, ran into trouble at the Troy Diner. According to Benny, some country bumpkins were threatening to beat him up when he left the diner, and he called in the cavalry, which included a half dozen fraternity brothers and me.

As we entered the diner, Benny was sitting at the counter. He quietly nodded in the direction of table where the gang of five yokels was sitting. We all split up, sitting in different spots, pretending not to know Benny.

With us to back him up, Benny finally found his balls and decided to challenge theirs. He slowly spun his seat around toward them and sneered, "Hey, you assholes, you still want to fuck around with me?"

At that, two of them got up and started walking toward Benny. I stepped in front of one of them and goaded him. "What's your problem, punk?"

"It's none of your fucking business, asshole. Get out of my way!" he grumbled, trying to push me aside.

At that, I grabbed a hot cup of coffee and threw it in his face, then landed a short right that knocked the screaming big mouth to the floor. Benny hit another guy over the head with a ketchup bottle, and dining implements started flying across the diner. The three remaining mountain men tried to come to their buddies' rescue but were kept pinned down by the other six brothers.

The melee lasted about three or four minutes and Benny got his justice. When the Troy police arrived, the bumpkins were in the corner licking their wounds and we were congratulating ourselves at the counter. There was a big discussion between the cooks and cops over whether to press charges against us or just make us pay for the damages. An amount was settled on, and the mountain boys split their share while Benny covered ours. He had deep pockets compared to us college kids and appreciated our backing him up.

After everything was settled, we went back to the frat house and mellowed out over a couple of beers. While quaffing down some suds, I pulled my close buddy Bob aside and confessed, "I don't know, brother. I'm beginning to get tired of getting into fights and getting into trouble over them. Everyone expects me to step in all the time and I don't know if I want to do it anymore."

Bob put his hand on my shoulder and smiled, "It's fine, man. You don't have to be that person anymore. You can change." He patted me on the back and walked off to get another beer. I looked around the room, watching the brothers who were at the diner gleefully tell the tale of what happened earlier that evening. I couldn't help but smile when the brothers started cheering for me when they heard about my coffee-in-the-face move. As I drove home I realized that, despite the trouble, sometimes I liked being the tough guy. I appreciated people looking up to me—at least it made me feel like a somebody.

In June 1970 I graduated from Hudson Valley Community College, and the following fall I started taking history classes at Albany State University. I also got a job working at Porter's Grill and was quickly made head bartender after my friend Paul left to work at a bar near the university. I got into the habit of patronizing his establishment between classes. It wasn't long before I stopped making it to classes and dropped out of school. That was how I ended up concentrating on my bartending career by default.

Without classes to break up my drinking, my marriage broke up. Wilma finally got fed up with me being drunk, hungover, or missing in action. On a cloudy October day, she scooped up Katie and left the farmhouse. A few days later the Sheriff paid me a visit. He told me I had to get out of the house that I had just bought from Wilma's father six months earlier. I didn't take the news too well and had to be forcefully removed from the house. I did end up getting money for the house, but the support payments nearly killed me. A family court judge decided that I should give $65 out of my $95 weekly paycheck to Wilma. It was a good thing that she lived way out in the country, because when I got real drunk—which was most of the time—I wanted to choke the life out of her.

I petitioned the court to lower my payments and when I finally got my day in court, I showed up wasted. I had been partying all night and hadn't slept at all.

"Where's your lawyer, son?" was the first thing the judge asked.

Making sure that everything got off to a good start, I responded, "I didn't want to pay him to go in the back room with you and her lawyer to figure out how to screw me."

Things went downhill from there.

When I snapped at Wilma's lawyer for saying something I didn't like, he warned me, "You're going to need a lawyer now."

"And you're going to need a doctor!" I barked back, setting off a commotion in the courtroom.

"Order in the court!" shouted the judge as he hammered his gavel.

Things calmed down for a short while until her lawyer came at me again and I told him, "Forget the doctor, just pick out a plot of land."

"Did you hear that, Judge? He just threatened me!" whined Wilma's lawyer.

"Wuss," I muttered under my breath.

"Mr. Broom, you either keep quiet or you will be going to jail, now!" threatened the judge. Somehow I found the power to keep my big trap shut and the judge dropped my payments down to $35 a week, but even this victory wasn't enough. Enraged, I followed Wilma and her attorney out of the courthouse. He noticed me following them and began acting as if he would protect her. That pissed me off even more.

"I'll show you, asshole!" I fumed as I jumped in my car and started following them as they walked down the sidewalk. I was literally driving on the sidewalk, chasing them down in my Chevy Vega. When I started to speed up, they ducked into a doorway so I missed them. I pulled back out into the street and raced over the Hudson River into Albany county where I went home to pass out.

Two days later the phone rang and it was the Troy police. The detective told me I could either come to the station or someone would come to get me. When I turned myself in, I was brought before the same family court judge. Sober this time, I was much more subdued and the judge just gave me a slap on the wrist. I had to promise that I wouldn't do anything to Wilma or her lawyer. I guess he knew how emotionally distraught I was, and it seemed like I had pulled myself together. Little did he know.

Chapter Eleven

I WAS OFFICIALLY A TRAIN WRECK. ON AN ENDLESS bender, I was out every night with a woman—or looking for one—and dogging every waitress and customer I could get my paws on. One such customer was Virginia. The sex was so good we decided that we shouldn't let her husband get in the way of it. His name was Nestor and she called him Nes. She called me Daddy.

We had a lot of a fun for a while, until Nestor found out about us and began to hunt me down. While I knew I could stand my ground, I was worried that he would catch up with me when I was too drunk to defend myself. The word on the street was that he was a giant badass who had already taken down some other tough guys around town.

It was about 2 AM in the morning when our paths finally crossed in the Fall Down Lounge. I was talking to a cocktail waitress when a 280-pound blockhead threw the door open and came charging toward the bar yelling, "Get up, Broom!"

Before I could move, he punched me in the cheek. I immediately snapped back a hard left jab that caught him in the eye and spun his head around. I didn't follow up right away, hoping he would think better of fighting back, but within a few seconds he came after me and pinned me up against the bar. My feet found purchase on the bar footrest, and I pushed off hard, throwing him off balance. Shoving him with all my might, knocking over tables and chairs, I landed on top of him in a heap on the floor. I started wailing on his head with both fists, missing more punches than landing them because his huge arms were blocking some of my blows. When he tried to push my head away with his forearm, I took a chunk out of his arm with my teeth. Within two minutes, he quit—or I let him quit. Typically, a bunch of people would have had to pull me off him, but this time I knew it was my fault.

Adrenaline pumping, I walked back to the bar, finished my drink, and ordered another. Nestor pulled himself up and painfully trudged up to the bar, sitting down to the left of me. I took a swill of my drink and without even looking at him said, "If you fuck like you fight, no wonder your wife screws around on you." I expected him to snap, but he simply stood up and silently shuffled out of the bar. He never bothered me again.

My biggest concern at that moment was that I would be banned from the Lounge, but they understood I was defending myself and even commended me on my performance. The cocktail waitress performed just as well later that evening. Virginia got mad at me for biting her husband and stopped seeing me, with the exception of one last fling during my second marriage.

I continued to drink, fight, and screw as much as possible. I did meet a beautiful Jewish-Russian girl from New York and briefly tried to keep my act together. I put my best foot forward at first, acting nice . . . then I acted like myself. As soon as that happened, she gave me the boot.

Porter's also gave me the boot after I called in sick one night. I wasn't unemployed for long though. I got bored quickly and knew that my unemployment benefits weren't enough to cover my bills, let alone feed my habits. I picked up a job working as a bar manager at new restaurant called Hyannis. I started out by helping put the entire bar together, including putting up the shelves and setting up the bottles for speed. There were actually two restaurants, a bunch of banquet rooms, plus a nightclub in the venue, so we needed to be able to crank out drinks as quickly as possible.

As soon as we opened we were swamped, and I was working six days a week, ten to sixteen hour days. Not only did I work hard, I played hard. This led to plenty of drinking and a lot of amphetamines to keep me going. My days off usually amounted to twelve to fifteen hours of sleeping, trying to catch up on the rest I needed.

Because we were right across from the state capitol building in Albany, we ended up catering many events for New York State politicians. I worked a number of private parties for Governor Rockefeller, the Lieutenant Governor, Speaker of the House, Senate Speaker, and their flunkies. I couldn't believe that they only had a couple bodyguards and would fantasize about knocking some of them off. I didn't really want to hurt anyone, despite the fact that they paid for the parties with New York State checks. I just couldn't help thinking about how easy it would be to smuggle in a semiautomatic under the portable bar.

It wasn't just politicians that came through. All sorts of celebrities would show up. We hosted a party for the NFL where Joe Namath was supposed to show up. He never made it but Hall-of-Famer Bob Tucker did, along with Bart Starr, Frank Gifford, and Commissioner Dan Rozelle. I met all of them, but wasn't that impressed—or at least that's what I tried to make them think.

The most important guest to me ended up being the family court judge who presided over my divorce case with Wilma. I couldn't believe that he was there and walked up to shake his hand. "Thanks for not locking me up, sir," I chuckled.

"I noticed you an hour ago and have been watching you be the congenial host of this party," he said thoughtfully. "Why didn't this person appear in my courtroom?"

I smiled and told him, "I can't really answer that question."

"I like Dr. Jekyll much more than the courtroom Hyde," he said and walked away. I kept thinking about his words for the rest of the night.

It took eight months for me to burn out at Hyannis. I didn't quit—they laid me off for a reason I can't remember—but it was inevitable. I couldn't keep up that pace for much longer anyway. I went back onto unemployment and picked up under-the-table jobs when I could get them.

One such job was promoting an Oktoberfest weekend that was to be held in August. The hustlers running the event, Sid and Adge, were two party animals I knew from Hyannis. I couldn't believe they were willing to pay me to go around to all the bars in the area to hang up posters and talk about the beer-drinking contests. It was the perfect job for me because I was going to the bars anyway.

When the weekend of the event came, I was put in charge of the drinking contest, which entailed ten minutes of hardcore beer drinking. It was pretty simple: the man who drank the most in that ten minutes won the money and the trophy. Of course, by the end of the ten minutes, the winner and everyone who competed were very, very drunk.

About five minutes after receiving his trophy, the winner ran off to a porta-potty and threw up so violently that his uppers flew out and into the stinking hole. The winner, if you can still call him that, returned to me a despondent man, asking me how to get his teeth back. Using every ounce of self-control, I tried to keep a straight face and told him I would call the porta-potty company. I did and they told me the man could get his teeth back in three days when they finally pumped out the deep, dark, hole. The winner didn't want to wait, but he had no choice—and he continued drinking. From what I heard from the company, when he finally got his choppers back, he immediately washed them off and popped them right back into his mouth. It's amazing. No matter how low you feel about yourself, there's always someone out there who is a bigger mess.

I spent about five months collecting unemployment, working odd jobs, and partying like a rock star. It was during this summer that I met a real head-turner I'll call Debbie. (I'm probably still on her shit list, too.) She was tall, with brown hair and a great smile. We started seeing each other almost every day and had a lot of fun going out dancing, on picnics, and to parties. I was drinking like I wanted to drink and enjoying not having too many responsibilities.

By October Debbie and I had moved in together. We found a dumpy apartment outside of Wynantskill, a suburb of Troy. It was a one-bedroom hovel, but it was in the country and was quiet. Several of our drinking pals also lived in the nasty little complex, so we had company. The only problem with the place was the winding two-lane road leading to it. It became a nightly challenge to drive down it after a full day of drinking.

In need of more cash again, I found my way back to Wally's after seeing an ad in the local paper. Sandy Chu, the northeast supervisor for Wally's bars, hired me as a bar manager and I went back full-time, which meant sixty hours a week. I gave it my best shot because I wanted to impress Sandy and the rest of management. I figured I could eventually work my way into a job like his in another part of the East Coast. I ran the bar like it was my own and became a real company man. I learned a bunch of management tricks and within months my bar was bringing in the second highest revenue compared to more than twenty nearby locations.

I was feeling hopeful when the owner of Wally's summoned me to Newton, Massachusetts, to meet with him. Sandy told me that he was considering a couple different bar managers in the chain to become a supervisor. At that time, Sandy's territory was from Maine to Maryland, and a guy named Bob was covering Virginia down to Florida. The owner wanted to break the territories up three ways and add a new supervisor. Sandy would take New England, Bob would handle Virginia and Florida, and the new supervisor would handle New York down to Virginia. It sounded like the opportunity I was waiting for, and I was ready for a change.

Apparently, the owner remembered meeting me back in 1968 when I was working as a bartender right out of the army. He had come into the bar dressed shabbily, with an unlit cigar hanging out of his mouth, and I didn't know he was the boss. When he called me over to the bar and told me to get a haircut, I told him to get fucked. He brought up the incident at the beginning of our meeting and told me he had liked me from that moment on. The encounter proved to him that I had heart. We hit it off from there and I wasn't nervous at all. I left Massachusetts feeling as if the meeting had gone exceptionally well. Unfortunately, a gasoline crisis hit right after that, and the boss put the position on hold. I decided that I would do everything I could to stay in the running should the position open up again.

I worked constantly; we were open 365 days a year. Thanksgiving, New Year's Eve, Easter, and Mother's Day were hands-down the busiest days of the year. Everyone worked their asses off on those days, and we typically had all 1,080 seats filled at one time or another. You never stopped making drinks or washing glasses.

For Debbie's and my first Thanksgiving in the apartment, I decided to invite two of my bartenders and their ladies over for dinner after we all worked our ten-hour shift. Debbie diligently cooked our turkey while we worked. When we arrived from our shift, I proudly carried the bird, potatoes, vegetables, and gravy from the kitchen to the table.

"Oh, this is gonna be tasty!" I said, licking my chops as I began carving the turkey. After slicing a couple pieces off the breast, the meat began to turn pink, then red. I threw the carving knife down and turned to Debbie "What the hell did you do?"

Apparently, my little homemaker had broiled the bird so only the first inch of it was cooked. Upon further investigation, I discovered she had also left the gizzards, neck, heart, and liver in the plastic bags and pushed the stuffing into them. "Great job, Debbie," I said rolling my eyes. "And tonight's menu now features plastic-covered stuffing."

Debbie jumped up from the table and ran into the kitchen. I followed her in there and was ready to go off when I saw that she was crying. "It's alright, it's alright," I said and stroked her hair. "We'll just make the most of it."

I went back out to the table, apologized to our guests for the fireworks, and made sure that they got the cooked turkey. Debbie and I settled for the potatoes and veggies. It was a good thing I was so busy at work that day because I didn't even have a chance to drink that much. If I had, I probably would have been a real bastard to her. Things between us had a tendency to get volatile when I was stupid drunk.

One day, for example I came home in the early evening as drunk as a sailor. "What is wrong with you? Why do you have to do this all the time?" she started bitching at me.

"Shut up. I'm sick of hearing you yap, yap, yap. If you don't stop right now, I'll drop you off the damn balcony," I threatened. We were three floors up.

"Yeah right, you drunk! I can't believe anything you say," she called my bluff.

I promptly proceeded to the phone and dialed 911. "Uh, yes. A woman just fell off the balcony."

"You're so full of shit," Debbie said and continued her tirade unfazed until she heard the ambulance siren in front of the building. She finally shut up and stayed that way for a couple of weeks. The same scene happened months later. When the phone call didn't work, I did try to hang her from the balcony until the ambulance arrived. This led to another three weeks of the silent treatment. Personally, I appreciated the peace and quiet.

Another time we were arguing about something — probably my drinking — and I did something else to scare her off. I don't know what it was but she jumped out of her chair and escaped next door to her friend's apartment. After about a half hour, I calmed down and walked over to her friend's to try to smooth things over. I knocked on the door, but no one answered.

"C'mon, Deb," I yelled. "Everything's cool. I'm not pissed anymore. Just come home." I waited, but no one responded so I went back to our apartment. About twenty minutes later I heard a knock on the door. When I opened it up, two state troopers were there.

"Are you Richard Broom?"

"Yes," I answered, confused why they were there.

"We have to place you under arrest for attempted breaking and entering," said one of the troopers.

"What the hell are you talking about?" I retorted.

"The women next door called in the crime, sir . . ."

"That's nonsense!" I exploded, throwing my hands up in the air. "I just knocked on the damn door."

"We have to arrest you and take you in, Mr. Broom," the trooper responded, ignoring my plea.

"I'm not going anywhere!" I fumed and proceeded to punch one trooper in the jaw and kick the other in the head before slamming the door on them.

About fifteen minutes later there was another knock on the door. Eight state troopers were there to greet me. They all had clubs and were taping them to their palms.

"Are you the only ones they sent? You're gonna need more back up than this!" I mouthed off as I charged out onto the lawn to do battle. I lost, and lost quickly. All it took was one good blow with a club to my forehead to take me down.

With a split skull and blood pouring down my face, they knew they had to take me to a doctor so they tossed me into the back of one of their cop cars. While back there, I recalled that state troopers had to pay for their uniforms, while local cops got a stipend to get their uniforms cleaned. Sitting behind the steel screen, I started wildly shaking my head so my blood would splatter all over the troopers' uniforms. At first, they didn't realize what was going on. "I think he's snapping," said one of them.

"No, jerkoffs!" I laughed belligerently. "I'm costing you money. Now you're gonna have to pay to get your uniforms cleaned!"

"If you don't stop it right now, Broom, we are going to pull over and finish what we started!" the other trooper threatened me.

My skull was pounding so I obliged, and they took me into a clinic with my wrists chained to my waist and ankle chains on, as well. The doctor came in, took one look at me, and said, "You need to take the cuffs off, boys."

"Yeah, take the cuffs off. There are only two of 'em," I slurred.

"No way," they refused in unison.

The doctor pulled the troopers aside for a moment and then returned with a needle that released me into la-la land. After he stitched me up I went to the county jail. I only spent a few hours there after calling a bail bondsman, and walked straight to the bar as soon as I got out. With blood caked on my head, I tossed down a couple of cocktails and then used the pay phone to call one of my frat brothers to pick me up. The bartenders just stared at me, but I didn't give a shit. I just needed to numb my throbbing headache. As soon as my pal picked me up I went back to his place, showered, popped two hits of speed, and went off to Wally's to work three banquets that night. In an ironic twist of fate, I ended up hiring Wilma's divorce lawyer to sue the troopers for overreacting. For a couple grand, I got off with a slap on the wrist, and I dropped the lawsuit as part of the deal.

I vowed that I was done with Debbie and her drama queen behavior, but somehow we ended up back together and I married her a year later.

Chapter Twelve

I NEEDED TO GET AWAY FROM THE DRAMA FOR A WHILE. When Sid and Adge asked me to go to Tampa with them to run another Oktoberfest event, I jumped at the chance. My job was to set up and maintain the beer stations where Beck's was going to be on draught for the first time in America. It was a groundbreaking, historical event; I knew I was destined to be a part of it.

Not only was I getting paid $100 a day, Sid and Adge also covered my flight, hotel, car, food, and drinks. In exchange, I was happy to work a good twelve hours a day, as I was still able to fit in another six hours of partying on top of that. I came prepared with some amphetamines I got from a shady doctor in Troy. Dr. Feelgood kept me alert even though I was drinking around the clock. I found a blonde squeeze at the Holiday Inn who kept me up as well. She also got me into trouble with Debbie by answering the telephone in my motel room while I was in the shower. I didn't care. I was making money and having fun in the sun.

The opening day of the ten-day event drew 20,000 people, and the next day another 25,000 people showed up. Things slowed down after that, with only 5,000 he next day and less than 3,000 the day after that. To minimize the damage, Sid and Adge closed shop and sent us home early. As I left Tampa I realized how much I liked having a pocketful of cash, and I resolved to find a way to make more money.

When I returned to New York, opportunity knocked. Gary, a guy I worked with at Wally's, asked me if I wanted to open a bar with him. It sounded like a brilliant idea. I had been drinking every day since I left the army, and now I'd finally be able to drink wholesale. Of course, I didn't have the money to pay my share for the bar or the liquor license, so I gave Mom and Big Bob a guilt trip and they bucked up. With that, the Locker Room opened its doors. It was a simple neighborhood bar, but I had big plans. My goal was to open a chain of gin mills around New York so that eventually I wouldn't have to work anymore.

In reality, the idea was ludicrous, and my first clue that I wasn't becoming a millionaire came on opening night. I was still working at Wally's, so after a nine-hour shift there I went to the Locker Room and made drinks for four hours straight. At the end of the night we had only taken in $300. Worse, it ended up being the busiest night we ever had. I figured out right away that it wasn't going to be the windfall that I was counting on. Still, I gave it my all. I worked on Sundays, my one day off from Wally's, and was there every other day of the week as well. During a two-year stint I only had three days off—not three vacation days, weekends, or holidays, but three days total.

Owning the damn bar ended up costing me the promotion at Wally's as well. I was passed up for the supervisor position because my involvement with the Locker Room was seen as a conflict of interest. They thought I might order liquor for *my* bar off *their* ticket and assumed that every time there was a problem with the Locker Room, I'd be blowing them off. When I found out they hired someone who wasn't with the company as long as I was, it was the final straw. I started stealing from them and letting things slide—so much for being a company man.

I concluded that it was time for me to widen my horizons and find new sources of cash. My fraternity brother Benny always threw money around without any visual means of support. I saw him spend like there was no tomorrow while I had to pinch every dime. I wanted what he had.

What he had was a pot smuggling operation. He wasn't bringing in anything from outside the country, just from Florida to New York. I didn't know how much he was bringing in at first, but there was no doubt that he was a big shot. Years later I found out that he was moving at least three hundred pounds a month. He also spent time hanging around offtrack betting establishments and local bars all day with half a dozen guys around him. I wanted to be part of that network and have a pocketful of money—without having to bust my ass sixty hours a week to get it. Working at Wally's and the Locker Room was the perfect cover, too. I was in one bar or the other fifteen hours a day, so customers could easily find me. I began dabbling in supplying pot, taking bets, and making collections. Benny, also known as Hambone, didn't let me get too dirty with the pot, but he liked having me around for the muscle.

I also found my way into doing collections for Old Joe the Bookie out of west Albany. Old Joe was connected. He wasn't in the Mafia; he just worked for the organization. I, in turn, worked for him. All I had to do was harass a couple guys who owed Joe money for bets they lost. My services came at a cost, albeit a low one. I viewed it as an investment in order to get my foot in the door for possibly bigger paydays in the future.

In many cases, it was a simple case of acting. I'd show up with Joe somewhere, looking mean and eager to hurt someone. Typically, it would result in Joe getting paid without me even having to lift a finger.

Eventually I started going out on my own to do collections. My job was to communicate clearly to losers the urgency of paying off their debts. It was actually entertaining much of the time. When Joe asked me to scare—I mean talk—to a newly arrived Greek immigrant who owed him $900, I paid the fellow a visit at the Greek diner where he worked as a prep cook. I casually strolled into the kitchen, dressed for the part in my leather jacket, and leaned against the wall, watching a young guy cutting up celery, tomatoes, and other veggies. Although he was the one with the big knife, he was obviously frightened.

"Are you Stavros?" I asked as I snatched a piece of celery and popped it in my mouth.

"Yes," he answered nervously.

Keeping my eyes on the knife, I coolly explained, "I'm a representative of Joe's and I'm looking to collect his $900."

Stavros was trembling and started rambling in broken English, "I have no money! I take long to pay back. Me make only $2.50 an hour." He was getting excited and kept talking with his hands and I continued to keep my eye on the knife. He wasn't threatening me with it, it just happened to be in his hands.

"Well, we can't wait for months while you pay $20 a week. If you won, I'd be paying you right now." I walked around the counter and put my hand on his shoulder. "Joe expects to be treated with respect and to be paid his winnings. I want all the money within two days, understand?"

Young Stavros yelped in a high-pitched voice, "I haven't got it! What are you going to do—kill me for $940?"

"No," I smiled. "I'm not going to do anything. I'm a good guy, but if you don't pay you'll be visited by someone not as nice as me." With that, I took another piece of celery and walked out.

Two days later, Joe called to tell me Stavros paid up. The owner of the restaurant witnessed the commotion and confronted Stavros

READER/CUSTOMER CARE SURVEY

HEFG

We care about your opinions! Please take a moment to fill out our online Reader Survey at **http://survey.hcibooks.com**.
As a **"THANK YOU"** you will receive a **VALUABLE INSTANT COUPON** towards future book purchases
as well as a **SPECIAL GIFT** available only online! Or, you may mail this card back to us.

(PLEASE PRINT IN ALL CAPS)

First Name	MI.	Last Name
Address		City
State	Zip	Email

1. Gender
- ☐ Female ☐ Male

2. Age
- ☐ 8 or younger
- ☐ 9-12   ☐ 13-16
- ☐ 17-20 ☐ 21-30
- ☐ 31+

3. Did you receive this book as a gift?
- ☐ Yes   ☐ No

4. Annual Household Income
- ☐ under $25,000
- ☐ $25,000 - $34,999
- ☐ $35,000 - $49,999
- ☐ $50,000 - $74,999
- ☐ over $75,000

5. What are the ages of the children living in your house?
- ☐ 0 - 14   ☐ 15+

6. Marital Status
- ☐ Single
- ☐ Married
- ☐ Divorced
- ☐ Widowed

7. How did you find out about the book?
(please choose one)
- ☐ Recommendation
- ☐ Store Display
- ☐ Online
- ☐ Catalog/Mailing
- ☐ Interview/Review

8. Where do you usually buy books?
(please choose one)
- ☐ Bookstore
- ☐ Online
- ☐ Book Club/Mail Order
- ☐ Price Club (Sam's Club, Costco's, etc.)
- ☐ Retail Store (Target, Wal-Mart, etc.)

9. What subject do you enjoy reading about the most?
(please choose one)
- ☐ Parenting/Family
- ☐ Relationships
- ☐ Recovery/Addictions
- ☐ Health/Nutrition
- ☐ Christianity
- ☐ Spirituality/Inspiration
- ☐ Business Self-help
- ☐ Women's Issues
- ☐ Sports

10. What attracts you most to a book?
(please choose one)
- ☐ Title
- ☐ Cover Design
- ☐ Author
- ☐ Content

Comments

about what was going on. After Stavros confessed his stupidity, the boss, a distant cousin to the new arrival, lent him the money to pay off his debt. The owner didn't want any further scenes in the restaurant. All he wanted was to keep his new slave in one piece. I was quite pleased with the outcome. Justice was served and I got paid.

Another idiot I had to put in his place was a harness-racing driver named Leopold. Joe had arranged with him to fix a race and placed a large amount of money on him winning. Leopold double-crossed Joe and could be seen pulling back on the reins coming down the home stretch. When Joe approached Leopold after the race and started giving him a tongue lashing, Leopold responded by slapping Joe across the face. That's when I was called in.

The next day I headed up to Saratoga to pay a visit. Leopold was supposedly a big guy, about six feet four inches tall and 270 pounds—a good thirty-five pounds more than me—so I brought along Jackie D., a certified lunatic, to watch my back. Around 2:30 in the afternoon, we arrived at a bar Leopold was known to frequent. I glanced around the bar and saw six patrons, two of them women, and surmised that if anyone fit Leopold's description, it was a guy with a girl three stools down.

I moseyed up to the bar, ordered a couple beers, and started questioning the bartender. "You seen Leopold around today?"

"No," the bartender answered without making eye contact. I could see that he glanced at the big guy three stools down.

"Yeah, I need to talk to him. I'm a friend of Joe's."

"Now what are you gonna do, tough guy?" whispered the girl to Leopold.

I decided not to do anything that night. I just made sure that the bartender saw the .32 caliber revolver in my waistband and told him to let Leopold know that I was looking for him.

Later that week, I came back with Jackie and another guy named Artie. The bar was packed so I bought three beers and sent my boys out to ask some questions. I stood silently, surveying the crowd, leaning against the wall in my leather jacket.

"Look at that cocky punk!" I overheard one guy saying. "He's just standing there, looking around. We oughta take him right now."

His friend stopped him. "No, man. He might be packing." His buddy was right; I was packing and would have used my gun if I had to.

Jackie and Artie reported back that the target wasn't there. After talking to about ten people, they said the word was that Leopold was laying low. With that, my job was done for the evening. Leopold would know we were there. I would either call Joe or I would have to visit Leopold again and introduce him to a baseball bat.

Two days later, I heard from Joe that Leopold had come to his senses. He paid Joe a visit, begging for his forgiveness, and actually got down on his knees and kissed Joe's ring. I'm sure Leopold had spent some sleepless nights, but no one got hurt physically and now Joe had a driver in his pocket for as long as he wanted. I had done it again without spilling a drop of blood. I also got a kick out of the fact that three months later, the drunks at the horse bar were still talking about the hit man after Leopold.

There was no doubt that Joe was a pro at playing the game. There was one time that he called me in because a bookie in Syracuse wanted us to kneecap another bookie for screwing him out of some money. Joe asked me to drive to Syracuse to meet with the guy who wanted to hire us, flash a gun, get all the information on the target, and get the three grand for the job. As Joe talked about the job, I started to feel queasy about it. The churning in my gut disappeared immediately when Joe finished his instructions. He told me to take the money, drive back to Albany, and we would split the three grand. That was it.

Noting the surprised look on my face, he explained. "This clown is not going through proper channels. He knows he's supposed to have a sit down with certain people to get permission to have this done. Dick, you know the business of making money is the priority here and violence hurts business. We are going to teach this schmuck that he needs to play by the rules."

"You got it, boss," I said and off I went. I felt that I had finally arrived when I got paid fifteen hundred bucks for taking a day trip to teach someone a lesson. Joe passed away shortly afterwards and I shed some tears at his wake. He was a class act.

After working with Joe, I decided that gambling was for suckers and stopped betting. I didn't gamble again—except with my life. By now I was drinking all day, every day, and usually had a couple blackouts a week.

When Debbie discovered she was pregnant, she sat me down and pleaded with me to stop drinking. "I don't want my child around someone who's drunk all the time. Please, I can't live like this anymore."

She wanted me to go to AA. I told her I would quit drinking, but I wasn't going to any meetings to do it. I decided to show her, Mom, Big Bob, and everyone else that I could do it. I sobered up to save my marriage and to play the martyr for my unborn child. I didn't pick up a single drink, even though I was spending almost every waking hour in either Wally's or the Locker Room. The best part of not drinking was that it got everyone off my back for a while. Debbie thought I was done for good, but I knew that I would be drinking again sooner or later.

After ten weeks, Debbie gave me a reprieve for one night. It was my bowling league's banquet at the Locker Room and she said I deserved to have one night of fun. I did, but a funny thing happened. Even though I had sixteen to eighteen drinks, I didn't get anything out of it. I didn't get high, I didn't catch a buzz, and I definitely didn't get drunk.

The next day Debbie had some questions. "How do you feel?"

"I feel fine. The party was good."

"How much did you end up drinking?"

"About ten drinks," I lied.

"Do you want to drink today?"

"No, I don't feel like drinking today. Relax. I'm not going to drink today, tomorrow, or whenever. I'm fine." With that I gave her a peck on the forehead and left for work.

I kept my word for another two weeks and then fell off the wagon—hard. Once again I was getting almost falling-down drunk every night, like I was making up for lost time. Debbie was heartbroken, but I didn't care.

Soon after I fell off the wagon, my second daughter, Erin, was born. The night Debbie went into labor, I stopped in a dive bar across the street on my way to the hospital. I knew everyone in the bar and, being the big shot, I bought a celebratory round for everyone, then another and another. By the time I staggered over to the hospital, my second daughter was already born.

Chapter Thirteen

WITHIN A FEW WEEKS AFTER ERIN'S BIRTH, I WAS no longer a bar owner. Big Bob found out that we owed the state money for sales taxes, got pissed off, and pulled the plug. One afternoon he came into the Locker Room and said he was selling the bar in two days. I was actually relieved at that point. I was doing everything I could to make it work, but it wasn't working. I was tired of saying "It will turn around," and of busting my ass between jobs while my partner never did shit. My only concern was what my friends might think. I couldn't even run a bar successfully. Everyone knew that the bar was in a depressed section of the city, but I still felt like a failure.

Ever since I fell off the wagon, Debbie was acting distant. I knew why but decided that it would be easier to get some loving elsewhere than listen to her bitch at me. There were plenty of opportunities for action while working at Wally's. Of course, you also never knew what you were stepping into there.

One night, Sid the promoter rolled in with two women—neither of them his wife. "Hey, Dick. I'd like to introduce you to Layla and Star," he said as he kissed each one on the cheek.

"Greetings, ladies. What can I do to you—I mean for you?" I joked.

"How about a round of shots? Maybe some Tequila?" Sid asked as he started to give Layla a back massage.

"I'm in," both Star and I said in unison. I winked at her and went to grab the Cuervo.

Several shots later, Sid split with Layla and I took off with Star. We picked up some salads and steaks and went back to her apartment. When she opened the door, I stifled a laugh. On her ceiling was a map of the heavens, and her bookshelf was lined with books on astrology. *With a name like Star . . . go figure,* I chuckled to myself.

After unloading the groceries and popping open a bottle of wine, Star grabbed my hand. To my disappointment, it was only to read my palm.

"Uh, oh," she said, examining my hand even closer.

"That's not what I want to hear," I quipped.

"You're missing a line here. Wait, okay, okay. Oh, wow." she sounded concerned.

"What?" I was beginning to get annoyed.

"I'm not sure, but I think the separation in this line means you're going to die young."

"Great. Just put me out of my misery," I grumbled as I reached for the bottle to pour another glass of wine.

"Wait. When is your birthday and at what time were you born?" she pressed.

After telling her, she grabbed a giant book off the shelf along with some papers, said she'd be right back, and ran into the bedroom, slamming the door. Not sure what to do, I started to cook up the steaks and polish off the wine.

About ten minutes later, she came rushing out of the room. "Get out!" she yelped.

"What?" I asked, wondering if this insanity was worth a quick lay.

"I want you out of here, right away!" She grabbed my coat and started shuffling me toward the door.

"What the hell is wrong with you?" I grabbed her arm.

"You aren't going to die when you're thirty-six. You're going to kill someone. Now get out!" With that she shoved me out the door. I stood there in the hallway, stunned, as I heard her turning the deadbolt.

"Crazy witch," I growled. I staggered to my car and went home to pass out on the couch alone. Little did I know that she was dead-on.

My drinking escalated even more after that. Everyone—Debbie, Mom, Big Bob, and the rest of the family—was disgusted with me by this point. But I just avoided them all by keeping busy at Wally's, helping out Benny, and working for Joe's people. With fall came football and making collections on bad bets, which fueled my ego and provided plenty of cash to feed my never-ending buzz.

One night in late October, I found myself in the Timber Inn after work, where I ran into another hothead, Pete. He was ten years my junior, but we had plenty in common. He had a lot of anger and a tendency for finding trouble. His dad was a well-known politician, however, and had the power to get him out of hot water when necessary.

After hitting a few watering holes in Troy, Pete and I finally landed in the same bar I went to after getting bailed out for attacking the state troopers a few years back. The joint was packed, but we found ourselves two seats in the middle of the bar and started drinking. Shortly after we were served, a group of guys came in and started showing off some judo moves they had learned earlier that night.

Pete decided they were creating a disturbance; they didn't seem to appreciate his perspective on the matter. We looked at each other and, without a word, waded through the judo club throwing punches. As the brawl escalated I wielded a bar stool to knock out a couple more guys, and then we took off for my car, which was parked half a block away. Four of the judo lads, now bleeding, chased us to the car. For some reason I had a starter pistol in my backseat. I grabbed it and pointed it at the posse now just ten feet away. "Keep coming, assholes," I challenged them. "I haven't shot anybody in over a week!" The lads, not fully fortified with alcohol yet, made the rational decision to back off, and Pete and I sped away.

We continued bar hopping. Two hours later we were getting into my car when we found ourselves surrounded by the Troy Police Department. Once cuffed, they searched my car and pulled out the unloaded starter pistol. With that, we were brought into the station and interrogated by the desk sergeant. He was talking down to us which riled me up even more. Pete transformed into an upstanding citizen, giving him the "yes sir" and acting like a wimp. Naturally, I did not.

"Screw you, asshole," I yelled. "I don't need you talking to me like this. Who the hell do you think you are, you pathetic piece of shit?" Then I leaned over and spat in his face. I was promptly shut up when the sergeant smashed my face into his desk. As I tried to break away from him unsuccessfully, I sliced my wrists on the handcuffs.

Pete dropped his daddy's name and was released, but I was held until the day shift came on duty. After I bailed myself out, they let me use the phone to arrange for a ride to the pound to get my car. I picked up the phone and dialed Debbie. "Hey, Deb. Uh, it's me. I had a little run-in last night."

"I heard," she said curtly.

"Well, I need you to come pick me up."

"No."

I rolled my eyes. "Listen, you have to come get me so I can get my goddamn car, clean up, and get to work."

"No."

"What do you mean, no?" I barked.

"It's over. We are over. Don't even try to come home because I have a restraining order against you. If you show up here you will be right back behind bars."

"You bitch," I muttered under my breath as I pounded my fist against the wall. "How the hell did you arrange that at four in the morning?"

"I filed for it over a month ago," she said matter-of-factly. "I was just waiting for you to get into trouble again to put it into effect."

Her smugness made my blood boil, and I resolved to find a way to teach her a lesson she would never forget. "Well, I need some damn clothes," I said.

"I'll drop them off at your parents' house," she answered icily and hung up the phone. I banged my head against the wall as I thought about having to return to Big Bob's. With no other options, I did just that.

Desperate to escape my parents, I started crashing at my bartender's house. He had just separated from his wife as well, so we were both in great shape. I kept trying to go home, but Debbie had the upper hand and stood her ground. She told me I could come back once I joined Alcoholics Anonymous and stayed sober for three months. My offer was to move into the house and then try to sober up and go to meetings. Neither of us gave in, so we gave up.

I also ended up having to go to trial for my big adventure with Pete. I was initially charged with a DWI (driving while intoxicated), but managed to get it reduced to a DUI (driving under the influence). I didn't have to do any time, but my license was restricted: I was only supposed to drive back and forth to work and to the grocery store. I didn't exactly follow that mandate, but was much more careful when behind the wheel.

The whole headache cost me even more money than just the standard legal fees and fines because I had to pay for a ten-week treatment program for the DUI in order to get my license back. Without any other options, I went to the sessions and played their game along with a bunch of other pissed-off people. Of course, it didn't slow my drinking down much. In fact, before going to my first class, I strategically tossed down four drinks. My rationale was that if I didn't drink that night, and then drank later on, the counselors would notice the difference in my personality. Ergo, I would drink before every class for consistency's sake—brilliant! I strategically drank vodka because, like all experienced drinkers, I knew that it had no smell.

About two weeks before the Super Bowl, our counselor requested that we start keeping a journal of what and when we drank each day. I bullshitted my way through, listing a glass of wine with dinner one evening and a few beers watching TV another night. On Super Bowl Sunday I was almost honest. I wrote down that I had fourteen drinks that day, when I really had over thirty—not counting what I had before going out to watch the game.

A few days later the counselor asked us to read our logs to them. When it was my turn, I shared my phony log. When I told him about Super Bowl Sunday, he stopped me. "How did you feel?"

"Scared," I replied.

The counselor seemed excited, as if he was witnessing some sort of breakthrough. "Why do you think you were afraid?" he gently asked.

Immediately bursting his bubble, I laughed. "Because the guy driving was drunker than me!"

The counselor eventually told me that I was a first-stage alcoholic and I needed to go to AA. I wondered what he would have told me if he knew how much I was really drinking.

Still bitter over the separation, I was spending countless nights getting loaded and stalking Debbie. I would watch her from a distance, hoping that I would see a car in the driveway that didn't belong there. I wanted to catch her with another man so I could storm the house and be justified to break some bones.

I also moved in with one of my gangster buddies, crazy Jackie D., because my bartender buddy had kicked me out. Jackie was recently separated and living in a four-bedroom house alone, without a car or a job. It didn't take me long to figure out why his wife left him. He really was nuts. In fact, years later the courts diagnosed him with manic depression.

I realized that I had to make a change before Jackie drove me over the edge, so I hatched a plan to move to south Florida. Wally's was building two new restaurants there, including one in West Palm Beach. They were willing to transfer me, but they weren't opening up for another month, so I needed to find a place to stay until then.

Benny ended up providing me with the perfect solution. He had a summerhouse on the top of a mountain in the Catskills. It had a couple of drawbacks: it could take me almost an hour to get to work in bad weather, and there was no insulation, so it was usually about 59 degrees inside during the winter. The other issue was that one of the five bedrooms was used as a storage area for up to 600 pounds of pot. During the day, Benny and his cohorts were there to transfer the buds into one-pound bags to sell. The upside was that I could live there for free in exchange for babysitting the pot every night.

I decided to make a go of it and moved in until it was time head to Florida. It kept me out of trouble for a while: the long, winding road up to the house made me think twice about getting too drunk before heading home, and that prevented me from being wasted enough to stalk Debbie.

A month later it was time to move to sunny Florida. I decided not to tell either of my ex-wives where I was going. I would still send them money, but I would determine the amount, not a judge. I gave no consideration to how this might affect my two daughters. All I thought about was how I was finally going to be able to escape all my bad influences and start over. As far as I was concerned, things were looking up.

I was nervous as I packed the car with my worldly possessions—clothes, bowling balls, golf clubs, and a small black-and-white television. I only had about a thousand dollars and knew that I would have to find a place to live before I ran out of money. The restaurant was scheduled to open up two days after I got down there, and I was supposed to be the bar manager. It seemed as if I had everything lined up. At least that's what I kept telling myself on the drive down.

When I got there, I immediately went to the restaurant where Bob, the southern regional supervisor, greeted me. After exchanging the typical phony southern niceties, he informed me that I wasn't automatically going to be the bar manager. He explained that I needed to prove myself first. I tried to stay calm, but all I kept thinking was, *After working for the goddamn company for six and half years as the bar manager in Albany, I have to prove myself here! Fuck that!* Somehow I kept myself from snapping and decided that I would suck it up until I could find something else after getting settled.

A few months later, after trying to "prove myself" to management, a greaseball from Long Island who liked to pose as a mobster ended up getting the job as bar manager. This was the last straw and I finally quit Wally's.

At first it seemed like quitting was a blessing in disguise. I landed a job at a swinging place in West Palm Beach called the Orange Crate. It was a nightclub-restaurant with live bands most nights of the week. As night manager, I would come in at 5:00 PM and work until 4:00 AM, Fridays through Sundays. I would bring in $200 for those three nights, which was what I made for working fifty-five hours at Wally's. The additional perks of the job included plenty of waitresses and customers to take home and becoming well-known around town—so I always got free drinks when I went out.

As always, however, it didn't take me long to find a reason to be unhappy with what I was doing. I started feeling as if I was just a glorified babysitter. The day manager ordered everything, so all I did was watch over the bartenders. I also resented the fact that the regular bartenders were taking home between $400 and $700 a week. I wanted a new position there and got my wish a couple months later when the place was sold. The new manager decided that one manager was enough. I didn't have to worry about being a night manager anymore. I was suddenly demoted to working as a cook, making sandwiches for the lunch crowd. Two weeks later I quit.

My next career move was working for a seafood distributor. I started out by putting in orders for restaurants, fast-freezing fish, and riding a forklift in and out of a giant drive-in freezer. I eventually got to deliver fish to restaurants around the area. I tried to convince myself that I was gaining valuable knowledge about local fish, which would eventually get me ahead in the restaurant business in Florida. How else would a guy from Albany learn about groupers, snappers, and dolphins? After two months of this charade, one day I discovered a red line going up my arm after being stuck by a fish fin. Apparently, I had fish poisoning. The owners of the distributor sent me to a clinic and told me not to use their insurance. They would pay in cash. I didn't trust them, so I told the doctor that I was hurt on the job. He gave me a shot and some pills, and sent me home. When I returned to work, they asked me how much they owed me. I told them I filed a disability claim and the next thing I knew I was laid off.

As luck would have it, I bounced back right away when another distributor called and said he was in need of my services. It was a different business altogether, but one I was familiar with. The employer was Fritz, Benny's Florida pot connection.

My job interview was held at a nearby diner. As soon as I walked in, I spotted Fritz sitting in a rear booth, lighting up a smoke. Wearing a cowboy hat and sporting a mustache, he looked like the Marlboro man. Over burgers, he proposed that I house the mules who were driving his pot up to New York in "company cars." Fritz figured that having his guys stay at my house would be less conspicuous than having them stay at a hotel. My responsibility was to let them crash there and keep them entertained for a day or two. Without missing a beat, I told him that it sounded like the perfect job for me.

By this time I was living with a guy named Bart in what we affectionately called the Tree House. It was a two-bedroom house built on eight-foot stilts to keep it from flooding during the rainy season. It seemed like a cabin at a summer camp, with two-inch-thick wooden walls and no insulation. I thought it was cool, but in reality it was a dump. But it was the perfect place for Fritz's mules to hide out and wait for their calls to make pickups.

For the sake of security, we never knew exactly when the calls would come in. The less each person knew, the less the chance that someone would share a secret with the wrong person. Everyone was kept in the dark—from the owner of the shipload to Fritz to the drivers and right on down the line. Of course, we found a way to get out to hit the clubs and party.

Within a month, Fritz called to see if I could drive my own car up to New York. He had a small load, only 280 pounds, that he needed to move. The hitch was that it wasn't going to Benny. Apparently, there was a disagreement between them, and Fritz was trying to punish Benny by working with another dealer in the area.

While I had known Benny longer, I needed the cash and accepted the job. When I met with Fritz to pick up the load, I was greeted by his 120-pound rottweiler. "Down, Oberon!" ordered Fritz, and the beast immediately sat down and started panting, giving me the classic rotty smile.

"Whoa, looking pretty snappy there, boy." Fritz smiled as he acknowledged my three-piece suit. "Good start. You knew not to let your freak flag fly. That's lesson number one." He continued on, sharing other tricks of the trade. "Next, we need to jack up the rear air shocks before we load up the trunk. Once you put all that weight in there, it will be leveled off. Just remember to let the air out after you make the drop off."

I followed his directions and loaded up. Before I shut the trunk, he handed me a box of Bounce fabric softener sheets. "What is this for?" I asked.

"To cover up the smell. Just put a bunch of these over the load and no one will pick up the scent of the buds."

I laughed, "Alright, whatever you say boss." Minutes later I was on the highway driving back to New York. After years of traveling up and down the coast, I knew the drive inside out. I did follow Fritz's guidance on avoiding high profile spots like the Delaware Bridge and the New Jersey Turnpike. I cut through the sticks of Pennsylvania instead. It was a boring drive, but with almost 300 pounds of marijuana in the trunk, boring was good.

When I got to New York I checked into a Ramada, hooked up with my latest squeeze from before I'd moved, and waited for instructions from Fritz. The next morning the phone rang and I was told to head out to a farmhouse in the country, just west of Schenectady. A couple of longhairs greeted me at the end of the gravel road and got a kick out of my suit. "Nice threads, brother!" grinned the younger guy sporting a dirty John Deere hat.

"I like to travel in style," I quipped, and we all lugged the bales of buds into their cellar. After sharing a few beers, I took off to call Fritz and let him know that the Eagle had landed. He told me to wait a week to collect the cash and then drive back, keeping in contact daily.

While wasting time that week, I ran into Benny in one of my regular haunts. He wasn't happy with Fritz nor was he happy with me. I told him that it was just business and I had nothing to do with executive decisions. He cooled off but I could tell that things had changed between us.

After a week, Fritz's new dealers still couldn't come up with everything they owed him, so I collected what I could and headed back home. It ended up taking over two months for Fritz to be paid in full. In the meantime, he worked things out with Benny. While they got back on track, I don't think Benny ever forgot that I crossed him, and he blamed me for the disruption to his business. I felt a little bad but focused on the fact that I had clearly demonstrated my work ethic to Fritz. I had followed his instructions to a T, arrived in New York within minutes of my ETA, and proved my loyalty to him by taking on the job despite my relationship with Benny. Once again, I felt optimistic about a new, promising career.

Chapter Fourteen

TO KEEP BUSY BETWEEN DRIVES, I PICKED UP A JOB as the assistant food and beverage manager at a big hotel in Palm Beach Gardens. My experience as a bar manager and owner, and of course my recently acquired expertise with Florida fish, got me the job. I was sporting a three-piece suit to work everyday and back to burning the candle at both ends. To keep up with the crazy shifts, all-night partying, and runs up the coast on my days off, I was popping speed before my shifts at the hotel. It wasn't long before my manager came to the conclusion that I was coked up.

The real issue was that hotel management encouraged us to have a drink or two on the job to socialize with the guests. They actually condoned waitresses bringing me a glass of wine or a beer with dinner. Little did they know that after that I would head to the liquor room to get booze for the bar, and I would snag a drink from a party partial—liquor that was used at a party within the prior two or three days. Then I would hit the cooler, pop open a bottle of wine, take a couple of swills, and revisit it several times throughout the night. I continued this routine every night, except when I was responsible for overseeing a party or banquet. The irony is that it was on the nights that I wasn't getting wasted that my manager thought I was using drugs. He kept looking for an excuse to fire me, but I had a contract so it wasn't easy. He finally found his chance when I mistakenly overcharged a wedding party on a $9,000 bill. The father of the bride realized that I was off by $120, and although it was an honest mathematical mistake, I got canned.

Luckily for me, business picked up for Fritz and Benny at the same time I was laid off, so I just swung into high gear, driving even more pot up the coast. Over the next year or so, I kept busy traveling back and forth to New York, making deliveries and collections. Life was good. I was paying my bills, partying all the time, and living between sunny south Florida and upstate New York. Naturally, I had to make sure everyone else knew that I was the man. Whenever I'd come up to New York I would head to my old haunts and show off. People were already wondering why I was hanging out in dive bars outside of Albany in the winter when I lived in South Florida, and once I'd get a bunch of cocktails under my belt, I'd start bragging about what I was up to. I made myself out to be a big-time operator when I really wasn't much more than a mule. I knew enough to only talk to people who were probably already getting pot from Benny anyway, but it was still a stupid move.

It was easy to make stupid moves when I was drinking as much as I was—and I made plenty of them. One especially dumb mistake was giving a bartender in Albany a wad of cash to make a car payment for me. It was before I got my raise to $1,500 a drive, and I was behind on my payments. I didn't want to drive the car to the bank because I was afraid they might snag it: I was already behind by two payments. When the barkeep returned from the drop-off without a receipt, I was buzzed enough to believe that they really didn't give him one.

About a month later I was back in Florida, smoking a cigarette while lounging on the couch in my terrycloth bathrobe, when I looked out the window and noticed two large men checking out my car. Moments later I heard two sets of heavy footsteps coming up the stairs and immediately stuck my nine-shot .22 caliber revolver under my robe.

Before they reached the top of the stairs, I opened the door and greeted them. "Can I help you?"

"Are you Mr. Broom?" questioned Goon #1.

"The one and only," I replied.

"We are here to repossess your car," grunted Goon #2.

In my usual congenial manner, I said, "You ladies aren't taking my damn car anywhere."

"We're just doing our job, sir," said Goon #1, trying to calm me down. "You're three payments behind, and according to your agreement . . ."

"I just made a payment, you dumb shit," I interrupted him. "The car isn't going anywhere." At that moment, they caught a glimpse of the gun in my waistband.

"Okay, sir. We'll check into your claim," muttered Goon #1 as they quickly backed down the staircase and scampered off to their car.

Three days later, I woke up out of a drunken stupor at 3 AM when I heard a noise outside. After grabbing the same revolver, I threw open the front door and ran out onto the landing to see what was going on. When I found the same two goons next to my car, I started yelling at them, accusing them of trying to steal it. Without a thought, I opened fire on them, shooting three rounds into the front of my own car so they would abandon their mission.

"Move! Move! He's shooting at us!" yelled Goon #2 as he ran toward the street to escape in his car.

Goon #1 was determined to get the damn car and was already behind the wheel. When I heard the motor crank, I started shooting wildly at him. "That's my fucking car, you son of a bitch!" I shouted as I pumped a flurry of bullets into the windshield. When they didn't penetrate the glass, the goon backed the car out quickly and took off down the road.

To cover my ass, I proceeded to run back into my house to call the cops, telling them that someone had stolen my car. After putting me on hold for a few minutes, they came back and told me there was repo activity in the area that night. Nothing else was said—that night or ever. My 1977 Grand Prix was gone, and I was just nine payments away from paying it off. It was riddled with bullets, though, so in my mind I called it even. Fritz ended up coming through with a fifteen-year-old Mercedes Benz. It wouldn't go over sixty miles an hour, but I didn't care; it had wheels and I could keep making my runs to New York.

In between my trips, I drank all day long—I mean, starting as soon as I got up. Many mornings I'd wake up at 10:00 AM but stay in bed until noon because I told myself that as long as I wasn't drinking in the morning, I wasn't an alcoholic. So I would lie in bed sweating until the clock struck high noon. Somehow, I found a way to control myself when I had to make a run up to New York. I wouldn't drink at all until I was about 120 miles from my final destination. Then I would pick up a six-pack for the last couple hours of driving.

By this stage, I was trying to keep a lower profile when I traveled to New York. Some people had figured out that when I was in town, a large amount of pot came in at the same time. Benny picked up on this and probably also heard about me flapping my mouth, and he told me to knock it off. Now, rather than showing off in my old haunts, like the Timber, I started hiding out in motels and cabins in the Adirondacks, Catskills, and Berkshires.

I still tried to see my daughter Katie when I could. She was always so happy to see me and kept asking me to move back home. While I wanted to be there for her, I knew I couldn't afford to go back there for good. I had an in with Fritz, and I planned to continue working for him for the rest of my life.

Of course, at this point, I was convinced that I wasn't going to make it to forty years old anyway. I figured that either the cops would shoot me during an altercation or I just wouldn't wake up one morning because of alcohol poisoning. I wasn't exactly the picture of health. I started every day trying to gag down my first drink. I would pour a beer, gin and orange juice, or gin and tomato juice, and try to get it down. It usually didn't work the first time. I would immediately throw up and then get the runs. According to a nurse I knew, both were because of bile from a malfunctioning liver. I was sure that I wouldn't be around too long.

The one thing that kept me going was my illustrious career. I was well suited for the lifestyle and thrived on living on the edge. It made me feel important, special—especially when I realized that most people would never have the balls to do what I was doing. For example, my roommate Bart took one ride with me up to New York, and by the time we got back, he swore he'd never do it again. I'd asked him to come along because I needed to take a Plymouth Fury that had a problem with the starter. Bart was mechanically inclined, so I figured having him along would help in case the car didn't start somewhere along my journey. (Obviously, it wouldn't be wise to bring a car with over 300 pounds of pot in it to a mechanic.)

Bart had the weekend off and agreed to ride up with me for a grand, which was equal to what he'd take home for working a week as an engineer. As we loaded up the trunk, I could see him getting nervous. While he'd known what I was up to, he had never seen more than a nickel bag before. Within twenty minutes of getting on the road, he begged me to pull over because he had to puke. He was fine after that, but he was only willing to be behind the wheel for three hours of the twenty-three-hour drive. I wonder what he would have done if he had known the car was registered in a dead man's name.

Chapter Fifteen

IN EARLY MARCH OF 1982, FRITZ CALLED ME TO MEET him and a couple drivers at a Holiday Inn just north of "Fort Liquordale." We met up around 9:00 PM, caught a quick buzz, and then headed out to go bar hopping. Walking down the stairs from the second-level room, we saw an Oakland Park police car come to a screeching halt in front of the motel. A cop jumped out, pulled his weapon, and started screaming, "Get down on the ground! Now!"

I turned around and looked behind me to see who he was talking to. No one was there. "Are you talking to me?" I asked incredulously.

"I'm talking to all of you! Get down now!"

"This has got to be a mistake," I said calmly, but got down on the ground when I saw the cop nervously flailing his gun around.

"We'll see about that," barked the cop. "You boys match the description of some suspects who just robbed a bank, now get down and stay down!"

We later found out that he was completely full of shit. The truth was that an off-duty cop was working security for the motel, investigating some recent break-ins. When he saw Fritz come by on his Harley, the rent-a-cop ran his plates and found out that Fritz had a warrant out for smuggling. Fritz didn't even know about the warrant. The bank robbery line was just a ruse to get us down on our stomachs so they could arrest Fritz. The rest of us weren't in any trouble until they found the fifty grand that one of the drivers had stashed in his gym bag. Of course, we all knew what the money was for, but the only evidence the cops had was the money. They decided to bring us in for disorderly conduct.

Back at the station, they were talking all sorts of trash and high-fiving each other for making what they thought was a big drug bust. The smack talk stopped as soon as the city attorney told them that they couldn't arrest us for anything. A few days later, the charges were dropped. I sued the cops for false arrest, the driver got Benny's money back within a week, and four months later Fritz was found not guilty on the smuggling charges.

It often felt as if lady luck was on our side. On a routine trip back to Florida, I almost had a run in with Johnny Law at JFK airport. I found out at the last minute that I was supposed to fly out of Albany that day. In a rush to get to the airport and already half in the bag, I didn't have time to take the $85,000 I'd collected and roll it up like socks as I usually did. So I threw on an oversized sports coat, stuffed all the pockets with the cash, and shoved the rest in my carry-on bag. When I tried to switch planes in JFK, two security guards stopped me after going through the x-ray machine.

"Whaddya got in there?" asked the older guard.

"Money, sir," I answered confidently.

"That sure looks like a lotta money to me," the rookie guard jumped in. "What are you doin' walking around with that kinda cash?"

Without missing a beat, I lied. "I was just up in Albany for my brother's wedding. While I was there some buddies of mine got talking and came up with the crazy idea to buy a claiming horse down at Gulf Stream. They all forked over the cash and now I'm on my way to see a man about horse." The story was so ridiculous that they couldn't even argue with me. "Yeah, right. Okay, go on," and off I went to catch my flight back to Miami.

Upon my return to Florida, I found out that our landlady at the Tree House planned to double the rent on us. I'm sure it might have had something to do with the gunshots in the middle of the night, odd characters roaming the neighborhood, and the frequent sounds of loud sex permeating the night air. The poor old widow must have heard it from the neighbors and decided she needed to get us out.

Although he couldn't handle the actual drives, Bart still got a thrill out of how my cohorts and I spiced up his life, and he agreed to find another place with me. We decided to look for a house off the beaten track and found a concrete blockhouse in rural Lake Worth on several acres of land. It had one road in and out, so I could keep tabs on any traffic. On the north side of the plot was a neighbor's yard that could serve as a way out if I needed to escape by foot. It was a dream home.

Things started to change after the move. I spent more time drinking alone at home than going out to the bars. It was cheaper to drink there, and I had a half dozen women I could call if I wanted to get laid, so I didn't need to go out chasing skirts anymore. When I knew that I wasn't going to be driving for a couple weeks, I'd stock up with a case of gin, a bottle of dry vermouth, a gallon jar of olives, and a pint-sized jar of cocktail onions. Then I'd make myself a very dry martini, sit down, drink it very slowly—and continue that routine until I passed out. About four hours later I would come to and do it again: drink, pass out, come to; drink, pass out, come to, drink . . . until the case of gin was gone.

Not long after moving into the house, I bought a heavy bag and strung it up on a tree limb outside the front door. I told myself it was for boxing, but it was really for taking out my frustrations and hostilities when life didn't go my way. One night, I polished off a bottle of gin, stumbled outside, and began pounding away at the bag. I started punching it harder and harder as I thought about the mess I'd made of my life. Sure, I was making enough money to live on. I had a roof over my head, food on the table, and women whenever I wanted them. But I couldn't stop the drinking and even though I walked around like some kind of drug lord, I knew I was just a lowlife who was so fucked up I couldn't even be there to watch my daughters grow up.

Furious with myself, I staggered inside and put a .32 caliber revolver to my head. With my finger on the trigger, I realized that I didn't want to live, but I was afraid to die. My hands started to tremble and I threw the gun down. *I can work this out,* I mumbled to myself as I went to the stereo, put on the theme from *Rocky,* and went outside to beat the bag until I collapsed from exhaustion. That was my first thought of suicide, but not the last. It happened at least four more times over the next eight months.

One day while I was sitting around feeling sorry for myself, I met Lola, the hot Cuban woman who lived in the trailer behind our house. She was five years older than I, but she was really good looking, with a great body. Her schedule was also similar to mine. She was on call like me, except in her case she was working for an escort service. She was also a stripper.

From time to time, I'd get ginned up, summon her over to dance for me, and we'd have wild sex. I felt a little guilty for using her, and I would tell myself that I shouldn't have her over anymore. But two hours later I'd be calling her again. Somehow she thought we had a good thing going. She was obviously mistaken. She wasn't going to find a loving relationship with me. The only reason I was with her was because she made me feel like I still had it. She claimed to be crazy about me, but she was really just plain crazy.

On the rare occasions that I was off my martini kick, I realized I didn't want to be such a nasty bastard. I'd tell myself I wasn't going to drink anymore but of course that never lasted. I'd start gagging down my first few drinks and then hate myself because of my lack of willpower. This would lead to me heading out to the punching bag, calling Lola over, or occasionally playing with my gun. I was completely out of control and convinced I could do nothing about it.

As I spiraled downward emotionally, paranoia set in. I began having nightmares about being in the house, surrounded by the cops, and having a shoot-out with them. I'd spend my days on the lookout, neurotically peeking through the blinds and suspiciously watching cars driving by when I went out to the mailbox on Davis Road.

One afternoon, I discovered that the toilet had stopped flushing. By that time, my bodily functions were so severely out of whack that it was a major crisis in my mind. Immediately, I ran for the phone to call my landlord. "Gary, we've got big problems over here," I said, pacing around the house with a martini in my hand.

"What's the matter?" my landlord asked nervously.

"The goddamn toilet isn't working!" I exclaimed.

"That's it?"

"What do you mean 'that's it'? How the hell is a guy supposed to take a dump?"

"Alright, alright, Dick," Gary tried to calm me down. "I'll call a plumber to come fix it right away."

"Thank you!" I said and hung up the phone, almost missing the receiver. I slammed down the rest of my martini and went to pour another one. I continued to polish off the gin, eventually passing out with an unlit cigarette hanging from my mouth. A knock on the door woke me up. Disoriented, and sitting in the dark with half a drink in my hand, I jumped up, spilling the martini down my shirt.

I opened the door a crack, then opened it a little bit further, and greeted the man at the door with a 9-millimeter automatic.

"Whoa, whoa, whoa! I'm the plumber your landlord called," he tried to explain. Seeing me swaying back and forth with the gun still in my hand, reeking of gin, he took off without a word.

Wasted, I simply shuffled back to the couch and lit up a smoke. An hour or so later, the phone rang. It was Gary. "What the hell happened, Dick?"

"Some guy comes over in the middle of the night, and I don't know who the hell he is. I thought he was trying to break in," I slurred.

"He knocked on the door, Dick. And it was only 7:30 at night."

"Yeah, well, that's later than I thought he'd be here. You should've called me to tell me what time he was coming,"

"But you're the one who . . . " Gary started to argue with me and then just gave up. "So now what do you want me to do?"

"Get the goddamn toilet fixed!" I yelled.

"I'll come over with another plumber tomorrow, and we'll be sure to call before we show up. See you then," he said, hanging up the phone, muttering under his breath, calling me a crazy son-of-a-bitch. *Slumlord,* I thought to myself as I leaned back and finally lit my smoke.

While my paranoia was primarily fueled by my drinking, there were legitimate reasons for those of us in the pot business to start worrying in early 1982. The U.S. Air Force lent the Drug Enforcement Agency (DEA) some AWAC (airborne warning and control system) spy planes to fly over the Florida coastline to track down planes and boats that might be smuggling marijuana and cocaine into the country. Before 1982, larger boats brought in tons of pot and loaded it off onto smaller boats ten miles offshore. From there it was rushed into various inlets. Most of the coke was brought in the same way, with additional shipments flying in on small aircraft from Columbia and an island in the Bahamas. Everything came to a screeching halt when the spy planes came onto the scene.

Fritz called a meeting with me and two of Benny's representatives to come up with a new game plan. Unfortunately, the plan consisted of doing nothing until things cooled off, which meant that I was out of work. I was living load to load, like normal people might live paycheck to paycheck, so I was screwed. I needed to find a job, but one that I could easily blow off once things got flowing again. I hadn't worked a real job in over a year, and I wasn't thrilled about the prospect. Pissed off and delusional, I started fantasizing about how to sabotage the AWACs while they were on the ground.

When I realized I wasn't going to be able to pay for my rent or my gin, I got a gig working as a bodyguard for another dealer in Miami. It was a short-term assignment; he needed someone to watch his back for a couple of days. Apparently he'd pissed off some other folks in the business and they had it out for him. I figured that I could turn the job into a networking opportunity and maybe find another source for Fritz.

I took the job for $250 a day, and by the third day I wished I hadn't. I was walking down the street with the dealer when a Cadillac raced up, the windows opened, and someone opened fire on us with an Uzi. I pulled out my 9 millimeter and returned fire, emptying the nine-shot clip into the car. The dealer pulled out a .357 Magnum, but just stood there, frozen. I grabbed it from him and fired it at the car. Somehow, neither of us was hit and within fifteen seconds the car took off down the street. Concerned that they might come back, I tried to reload the clip I'd just emptied, but my hands were shaking so much that I was having difficulty doing it. Stucco and concrete chips from the surrounding buildings flew everywhere during the shootout, so I was covered in white dust from head to toe, looking as if I had a bad case of dandruff. A sane person would have quit the job on the spot, but not me. I wanted to make a deal with this dirt bag, although he wasn't willing to talk about moving any pot. Two days later, he let me go because he apparently worked things out with his associates in the Cadillac.

Without any drives scheduled for several months, I decided I should find another job, preferably not as a bodyguard. While at a pool party at my friend Martha's house, I found out that two of her friends, George and Matt, were taking over a topless bar called the Tender Trap Saloon. Formerly called the Purdy Love Pub, the saloon didn't have a liquor license and could only sell beer and wine. Of course, this didn't matter much since the real reason people came in was for the women taking their clothes off for minimum wage and some tips. Aware of my expertise in the hospitality business, Matt and George invited me to come and take a look at the place the day before they closed on it.

"So here is where the magic happens," Matt said proudly after giving me the grand tour.

"Wow, this place is something else," I smiled, stopping myself from telling him that it was a dump with a stage.

"Sure is and we've been thinking, we'd like you to be a part of it. What do you say about working for us as a bartender?" George asked excitedly.

I was caught off guard. Before I could respond, Matt added, "It would be great, Dick. We could really use you. You know the business. We'd put you in charge when we're not around."

"Well . . . " I tried to stall, not knowing how to respond. "Sounds like a promising opportunity. Let me sleep on it and I'll get back to you tomorrow." The next day I called them up and took the job. I was desperate for the cash and figured I could always pull out the "family emergency" excuse if Fritz needed me. The real selling point on the job was that I could drink while I was working as long as I didn't get falling down drunk. There was no gin there, only beer, and it took a lot of that to get me wasted, so it sounded like a feasible proposal.

A few days later, I joined the Tender Trap team, opening cans of cheap beer and pouring wine out of gallon jugs into plastic cups. It was a real classy joint. I couldn't help but wonder about how a year ago I was wearing a three-piece suit working as the food and beverage manager at hotel where there were 175 different types of red wine alone and now I was serving Old Milwaukee.

The lovelies I worked with were a handful, as well. They were constantly bickering with each other. I was put in charge a lot more often than anticipated, so I would be the one that they would complain to. They'd whine about everything, especially about stealing each other's customers. Joy would come up to me, in a silver bikini and plastic pumps, hissing, "Cherry's cheating! She keeps taking her panties off! Now Johnny comes into see her rather than me and that's not fair!" My typical response would be something like, "Johnny is a Tender Trap customer, and if you aren't making the kinds of tips that Cherry is, then maybe you should take your thong off too." No matter what answer I'd give, it usually led to a drama queen stomping off in a huff. The job got real old, real fast, but I tried to focus on the fact that I could drink twenty beers a day for free while getting paid enough to cover my bills and still have money left over to play.

About week four of my new job, I got a reprieve when Fritz called and asked me to make a run for him. I told the Tender Trap that my grandmother was sick and escaped for a few days. Five days later, I came back to the same nonsense, but with even less tolerance for it. The pathetic women with their biker boyfriends acting like managers drove me up the wall. A week later, I walked out and found myself yet again unemployed in June 1982.

Without anywhere to be everyday, I quickly slipped back into the drinking, passing out, coming to, and drinking again routine. About two weeks after I left the Tender Trap, I met up with Fritz in Fort Liquordale for a couple of cocktails. We caught up at a bar along a canal. Fritz rode his boat up to the dock, and I'd driven one of the company cars, a 1979 Buick Electra. We had a few drinks and the next thing I knew, I woke up in a shabby motel room. Sitting up in bed, I looked around for clues to what had happened. There were four ounces of wine left in a quart bottle on the nightstand and three full beer cans on the dresser. I got up out of bed, opened the door, walked out onto the balcony, and looked around. Nothing resembled any part of Florida I'd ever been in before. I went back into my room, switched on the television, and waited for a station break. I didn't know what had happened, but still a last shred of pride prevented me from calling the front desk to ask where I was. After about fifteen minutes of watching the boob tube, I figured out that I was outside of Charleston, South Carolina.

I threw on some clothes and walked out to the car to check the trunk. I assumed that since I was off I-95 I must have been making a run for Fritz and that there must be a couple hundred pounds in the trunk—but it was empty. All I could find were twenty empty beer cans in the back seat. This was officially the worst blackout yet. I'd driven seven or eight hours and didn't recall any of it. I also had no idea where I was going or why.

Back in Florida, I continued to unravel. Although I hated working at the Tender Trap Saloon, I still found myself hanging out there a couple times a week—probably because I felt like a VIP compared to the regular customers since I used to help manage the dump. Lola still came around every once in a while, but I cut out the gin-fueled orgies with her. It might have been out of a sense of guilt for abusing her or that she was too clingy—or maybe it was because she was too crazy even for me. I had a collection of other women I was seeing, including Martha, when her boyfriend Cheech wasn't around.

During the days leading up to the Fourth of July I had nothing to do but drink. And that's all I did. I just stayed drunk, wishing that I were dead. So it wasn't surprising that on July 2, I found myself back on the couch, an empty martini glass in hand, with a .44 Magnum revolver in my mouth. After pulling the hammer back, I sat there and shook, but wouldn't take the gun out of my mouth. A minute later, I had an image of my mother yelling at me for ruining my teeth after she spent all that money on braces when I was fourteen years old. Laughing to myself, I pulled the barrel out of my mouth and stuck it to my ear. After holding it there for thirty seconds, I laughed to myself again, deciding that it would be much too loud and painful to my eardrums. Then I stuck the revolver up to my right eye and peered down the long seven-inch barrel. Seeing no light at the end of the tunnel, I pulled the gun away, released the hammer, and set the gun down on an end table. To no one in particular, I chuckled, "Fuck it. I'll just get drunk instead." I poured another martini and slipped into another blackout.

Coming to on July 4 around 10:00 AM, I turned on the television to find out what day it was. After crawling out of bed to grab a breakfast beer, Martha called to nail down our plans for later that day. She wanted to go to a party at the house of some astronaut who planned to run for Congress, and I didn't feel like going. I wasn't in the mood to act civilized. I wanted to whoop it up and raise some hell. I also didn't want to embarrass Martha, and considering my regard for politicians, it might not be a wise idea to take me to party with a bunch of them and then pump me up with drinks. The outcome would most likely be ugly. She tried to talk me into going, but after listening to me go off she finally agreed that I was probably in no shape to go.

Off the hook, I hopped in the shower, tossed down a couple of beers, and headed off to the Tender Trap. Arriving shortly after noon, I promptly started drinking, shooting darts, and carrying on. Later on, I made a quick run back home to get my .44 Magnum because over the afternoon I'd come up with the brilliant idea to shoot it off once the sun went down. I wanted to show the crowd some real fireworks and be the big man with the big gun. As the day turned to night, the darkness settled in and everything faded to black.

Chapter Sixteen

THE BARRED WINDOWS CAST A LONG SHADOW
across my cell as the sun slowly rose in the Florida sky. The
past few months of sobriety and reflection not only brought a sense
of clarity to my past, but to the harsh reality of the present. Since my
first drink, I'd always had a way to escape my cares. Now, sitting in a
prison cell, I was forced to face them head-on without anything to
dull the pain or wash away the fear. Although it was springtime in
Florida, a cold chill ran down my spine as I thought about what had
happened nearly a year ago.

Of course, I knew that it wasn't really my fault. Even Nanny
blamed Mom and Big Bob for everything in her letters to me. She
actually went so far as to write to my lawyer, Mike, to tell him how
they screwed me up. He fell for it, too.

A few weeks before the trial he called me in for a meeting to let
me know that he hired a clinical psychologist and forensic psychiatrist to interview me and then testify on my behalf during the
upcoming trial. He also explained that he was planning to argue that
I should be charged with second-degree murder rather than first,

because my drinking impaired my mental capacity: I wasn't able to formulate the intent to commit the crime. I knew it wasn't first-degree murder because I didn't even know the victim—or at least I didn't think I did. I hadn't even seen a picture of the guy yet, so there was a chance I may have seen him before that night—but I certainly didn't know him by name.

I was hoping for a manslaughter charge or even an acquittal due to temporary insanity because I was so wasted that night. During our meeting, however, Mike said that there might be a problem using the alcoholic angle because the guards at County claimed that they had never seen me go through withdrawal. I couldn't believe it.

"What do you mean they don't think I had a problem? They didn't see me shaking and sweating in my bunk for the first week I was here? Those guards don't pay attention to anything!"

"Okay, Dick, take it easy. I'm just trying to tell you," Mike tried to talk me down. "What I'm trying to tell you is that they never saw you drunk."

"So what are you saying—that I should get wasted?" I laughed.

Mike was silent.

"Are you serious?" I whispered to him.

"I can't tell you to get drunk," he said unconvincingly. "I'm just telling you that it could be a problem if the guards testify that they've never witnessed any signs of your alcoholism. Do you understand what I'm saying?"

"Loud and clear, boss!" I replied with a big grin on my face.

I immediately set off to brew up some buck. After acquiring a giant garbage bag, I began throwing anything with sugar in it: Kool-Aid, juice, pancake syrup, and whatever else I could scrounge up from the cafeteria. I traded my meat for sugar. I traded my milk for sugar. I traded my potatoes for sugar. Everything went in trade for sugar. After a couple days of gathering the sugar, I added slices of bread and rolls to the stew for yeast. On the seventh day, which happened to be Easter Sunday, I was blessed with five gallons of hooch that contained about 18 percent alcohol.

My game plan was to celebrate the holiday by quaffing down a couple drinks with a bunch of the guys in the cell block, Then, when the guards came through to check on us, I would let them catch the smell of the booze on my breath. If that didn't work, I would give them a real show.

The plan went out the window shortly after taking my first swill of the gasoline-tasting brew. Within minutes I was refilling my cup for the third time as a warm, familiar feeling came over me. I quickly changed my mind about sharing the buck with the five other inmates I'd promised it to. Realizing that my stash could keep me drunk for the next four days, I told Brian, "To hell with sharing the shit! This is just for us. Screw the brothers. They're not having any of it."

I checked the doorway that led from the big cell into the little cell where I slept. There was no door, but the opening was just two feet wide with vertical steel bars on either side. Deciding to hoard the hooch in the tiny cell, we began taking turns drinking and keeping the rest of the lads out. By keeping the bag in the toilet, it was just out of reach from the other inmates—who tried to grab it through the bars of the cell. For the next two hours I had a grand time, drinking, fighting, and feeling more and more like my old self.

Since it was a holiday, the jail was running on a skeleton crew. Those who were working didn't want to deal with us without enough troops to back them up, so they simply ignored the ruckus coming from our cell. Every once in a while, they would open the door and yell for us to keep it down, but they were too intimidated to come in and shut the party down.

Amid the fracas, one of the brothers, Eddie, kept trying to reach through the bars to fill his cup. He was a little guy, only about five feet, six inches tall and weighing maybe 150 pounds, but he had a big mouth. He was a pain in the ass, and I had been dying to bust his head open since he entered the cell block two months ago. The only reason I hadn't was because Mike kept telling me, "Don't show any violence. Whatever you do, just don't show any violence."

It was much easier following that advice sober. In the heat of the battle to protect my bag of booze, I grabbed Eddie's wrist and bent it backwards, breaking his right arm between his wrist and elbow. After letting out a screeching howl, he scurried away, trying to hold the broken arm together with his left hand.

The siege on our stash slowed down after that, allowing Brian and me to kick back and swill for a few minutes until a squad of correctional officers trained to quell riots came storming into the cell. Apparently, they were called in on their day off to deal with us and were pissed off about it. There was no resistance to their charge. Brian and I were half in the bag, and the rest of the guys were already fought out. Seven of the eighteen inmates of the cell were hauled down to the first-floor holding cells, and the guards snatched up the rest of my buck.

I found out later that the buck would have turned to vinegar within twenty hours if I didn't keep it refrigerated, so I wouldn't have been able to stay drunk for the next four days anyway. I guess that means I was a selfish pig for nothing, but screw the rest of the guys in the cell. What had they ever done for me except give me headaches?

After waiting in the holding cell for a couple of hours, I was finally brought in to see the captain who was in charge of the entire jail. Smirking at me, he asked, "Did you have a good time today?"

Still drunk, I grinned and proudly answered, "Yes!"

"I'm sure you did," the captain laughed. "I understand there was some wine up in the cell. Is that true?"

"Yes."

"Do you know whose wine it was?"

"Sure. It was my buck," I bragged.

Laughing again, the captain said, "Eddie's arm is broken. Do you know how that happened?"

"Of course I do!" I boisterously exclaimed. "I broke it when he reached for my buck!"

With that, the captain howled. "This is the first time that an inmate has ever been so truthful with me, Mr. Broom. I appreciate the honesty."

"No problem, Captain, " I slurred.

"Ha!" he chortled, amazed and amused by my audacity. Shifting to a more serious tone, he said, "Listen, we are moving you to a different cell block and everyone involved in this fiasco will be split up so that the fighting will stop. Just know that the officers didn't appreciate you interrupting their Easter dinners because of your wine."

"Sorry about that, sir," I mumbled over my shoulder as I walked out of his office and back to the holding cell.

An hour later I returned to my old cell to pick up my box of letters, police reports, and depositions. As I was escorted to a new cell, I felt an odd sense of loss over the move. It reminded me of being kicked out of my home during my separation from my first wife. While I was glad to get away from the aggravation, I somehow missed the familiarity of it all. Did that mean that this place was becoming the new normal? Fuck that! I realized that I had to find a way out of here.

The next time Mike came to see me, he wasn't pleased. Pacing back and forth, shaking his head, he berated me. "All I wanted you to do was to find some way to show them that you have a problem. I didn't expect this!"

"Did the prosecutor and judge hear about my little Easter Sunday fun?" I chuckled.

"Yes, Dick, they did. And it's no fucking joke!" Mike shot back. "Why did you have to cause such a big problem?"

For once, I was trying to calm him down. "I wasn't trying to cause trouble. It just happened."

"It always 'just happens'", he sighed as he collected his files and headed toward the door. "They certainly know now that you have a problem with alcohol!"

"Good," I said to myself as the door slammed shut.

For the next few weeks, I did everything I could not to think about the trial. I tried to keep my mind busy, making phone calls and reading, but I kept slipping into morbid reflection and projection. For example, while watching TV, thoughts of the trial would start creeping into my head. I'd picture myself in ankle and waist chains, walking down a long prison corridor surrounded by guards and a man in a suit. Awaiting me at the end of the hallway was Old Sparky, the electric chair. I'd try to block out the image and go back to watching the boob tube, but would find myself trembling as I did. The same images began to infiltrate my dreams as well. Lying awake at night trying to escape the dreams, I knew that the victim's family would be elated if they came true.

Chapter Seventeen

ON MAY 6, 1983, MY TRIAL BEGAN. I ENTERED THE courthouse feeling confident and sporting a three-piece pinstripe suit without the shackles. A couple of deputy Sheriffs escorted me to a table in the front of the courtroom where Mike was waiting for me. We made small talk for a few minutes until Mike leaned over and whispered in my ear, "Do me a favor. Turn around and check out the woman flanked by two guys in the back row directly behind you."

I glanced back and saw an old woman with two middle-aged men who looked like they could be her sons. "What about them?"

"Take a good look at the guy with the beard," Mike uttered under his breath, pretending to shuffle through his papers.

When I turned around again I met the angry glare from the bearded man.

"Do you recognize him?" Mike asked quietly.

"No, I don't know him," I answered, wondering what the hell was going on.

"He's the victim, Daniel's, brother, and he looks just like him," Mike explained, thoughtfully watching my response. "The woman is their mother."

When I turned again, they were all glaring at me and I understood why. They hated me.

A chill ran down my spine, but not because of the hate emanating from Daniel's family. Rather it was because I thought Mike was trying to trick me into admitting that I knew the victim. Obviously, he didn't believe my story about the blackout and thought I was lying. Meanwhile, he was the one who wanted me to say that the victim had a gun so I could plead self-defense. Even though it could have gotten me off, I wouldn't say it because I didn't want to lie. The truth was that I couldn't remember a damn thing that happened that night. Right as the prospective jurors started to file in, I came to the sickening realization that I couldn't trust my own fucking lawyer, even after giving him twenty grand.

Once all the prospective jurors found their seats, the judge and my number one fan, Nora the prosecutor, strolled in. After calling the proceedings to order, the judge explained that the first step of the trial was the *voir dire,* which entailed picking the jury. Both the state attorney and defense attorney would interview the prospective jurors in order to determine who would be fit to serve on the jury. Of course, each party was really looking for the jurors who would be favorable to his or her side of the case. Mike, my defense attorney, wanted the most liberal-minded jurors who were against the death penalty, while Nora wanted people who thought I should be hung from the nearest tree. Each side had a limited number of times they could disqualify possible jurors without a reason. Mike and Nora battled it out over a number of potential jurors. One of them was an ex-cop who would have been Nora's dream juror, but Mike blocked him from being selected.

The process continued until twelve jurors were picked along with two alternates who would sit through the whole trial and listen as if they were going to decide the outcome. Once selected, the jury members were given instructions by the judge, and the opening arguments were presented by the state attorney and then by my lawyer. Nora claimed that the jurors would insist on charging me with first-degree murder once she had the opportunity to show them how I had formulated intent to commit the crime. Mike acknowledged that I did commit a crime, but not first-degree murder. He wouldn't claim I was innocent, but would show that I was too drunk to formulate any intent. Whether or not the jury believed I had intent determined whether or not I would get the chair.

I initially thought that intent was the same as premeditation—making a plan and carrying it out. According to how the law was written, however, I would be guilty of intent if I walked out the bar door to my car to retrieve the gun and then came back in to use it. Even though it would only take a minute or even thirty seconds, that action would qualify as "intent." Based on all the depositions I'd read, I was confident that I had the gun in my belt. Therefore, as far as I was concerned, there wasn't any possibility of my being convicted of first-degree murder. At least, that's what I was thinking before Nora began presenting her case.

As Mike was wrapping up his opening argument toward the end of the day, I glanced back again at Daniel's family. When no one was looking, his bearded brother mouthed the words: "I'm going to kill you." I swung back around and pretended to focus on what Mike was saying, but had a hard time concentrating as I could sense the piercing stare coming from the back row. When Mike sat down next to me, all the color was drained from my face. "What's the matter?" Mike asked. "I thought I just gave a convincing argument."

"Nothing," I answered softly as I noticed the bailiff watching my every move. The judge had called it a day and two guards were waiting to escort me back to my cell. As I passed Daniel's family his brother mouthed the words again while patting his grieving mother on the back. Leaving the courthouse, I had a sinking feeling in my stomach and my confidence was long gone.

Later that night I was back in my cell reading a letter from Nanny, when one of the inmates came charging in and punched me in the eye. Instinctively, I jumped up and ran after him but somehow stopped myself before it was too late. I knew I couldn't get into a brawl, especially in the middle of the trial. Despite my uncharacteristic display of self-control, I still ended up having to walk into court the next morning with a black eye. Mike tried to explain what happened to the jury, but I knew the day was off to a rocky start.

Nora spent the day calling up an array of state witnesses—detectives, weapons' experts, crime scene investigators, and the coroner. Even the detective from New York who arrested me, Mr. Good Cop/Bad Cop, dropped by to lie on the stand.

It seemed as if Nora was testifying more than her witnesses. She would ask them a question, they would make a statement, and then she would elaborate on their answer. It was if she was just continuing her opening argument. I kept pushing notes to Mike saying, "She can't say that!" and "She's just making up a story—a fable full of her own ideas about what happened that night! Hell, even I don't know what happened that night!" Occasionally, Mike would object to her conjecture but she would start right up again with the next question. It seemed as if the whole trial was a show, a chess match, and my life was at stake. I didn't like the game but knew we had to play it to win.

Amidst all this, Daniel's brother kept up the threats. Every time I turned around he would mouth something or make some gesture. I finally decided to tell Mike, and he immediately informed the judge. Minutes later we were all in chambers and the judge was telling Daniel's brother that if he did it again, he'd be arrested for assault and barred from the courtroom. Furious, the brother stormed out; he did, however, keep himself in check for the rest of the trial.

Back in the courtroom, Nora called up a weapons' expert who ended up backfiring on her. After painting a dramatic picture of the .44 Magnum used in the crime, literally comparing it to a cannon, her weapons' expert began playing with the weapon as if it was a toy. Mike picked up on this, and during his cross examination he capitalized on the expert's giant ego and quickly got him to start twirling the gun around on his trigger finger. The guy even demonstrated how easy it was to cock and uncock the revolver. This clearly discredited the cannon comparison and Nora was fuming. I could tell Mike got off on riling her. Hell, so did I.

The next round of witnesses included people who were at the bar the night of the shooting. One of them was Daniel's friend who was visiting from up North. During the cross-examination, he admitted that he was drinking for hours before coming into the Tender Trap and couldn't identify me as the shooter. "I was so drunk that night that I couldn't identify anyone—except maybe a pair of tits!" he joked as Nora winced.

"Thank you for your time, sir," Mike said as he dismissed the witness. Grinning from ear to ear, he walked back to our table. "Listen, as far as I know, Red is the only witness who can testify that he absolutely saw you use the gun. The crime scene experts couldn't even say that the projectiles came from the .44 Magnum. The slugs retrieved were too damaged to match the striations in the barrel of your gun."

"Good," I responded uneasily. I still felt nervous about where things were headed. "Is Red up next?"

"No, not yet. We have to wait," explained Mike. I let out a sigh as Nora called up her next witness, Matt, one of the owners of the Tender Trap who was bartending the night of the shooting. He couldn't say much about the shooting itself, but he almost ruined our entire case when he said that he'd never seen me drunk before that night.

"He's never seen me sober!" I whispered to Mike. "He has nothing to compare it to!" Mike challenged Matt's view about my drinking problem during the cross-examination. Matt said he could certainly tell I was bombed on July 4, but always just thought I was a happy-go-lucky guy. Then he lost some of his credibility when it came out that the night of the crime he had told the cops that there wasn't even a shooting. Apparently, he thought it was all a prank— despite the blood splattered on the side of the bar. He thought it was chicken blood and the noise was blanks. Matt was convinced that there was no way I could actually have done what I did. Apparently, I had him fooled. Sitting there in the courtroom, I couldn't help but think about the irony of the situation. I spent most of my life hiding the fact that I had a drinking problem, and now my life depended on proving that I had one.

After a bunch of other witnesses, Red finally took the stand. He repeated his story about us comparing guns a few weeks before and talked about our good old times together drinking and shooting darts. Becoming impatient with his southern-style ramblings, Nora, who was probably originally from New Jersey, cut him off. "Great, so you knew each other. Why don't you tell me about what happened the night of the shooting?"

"Well, 'bout midnight a man came in and started causin' a commotion. I heard Matt tell him he had to put his shirt on and leave the dancers alone. He kept up his nonsense and continued pushin' around a couple of the regulars, and even gave Cherry, my favorite dancer, a hard time. Dick leaned over and told the guy to knock it off, and the troublemaker told him to go fuck himself."

"Then what happened?" Nora prompted him.

"Well, Dick pulled the .44 Magnum from his pants, stood up, and started swinging the gun around—first to my left where the jukebox was and then toward the middle part of the bar where the troublemaker was standing. I grabbed his arm to try to stop him from shooting the guy, but the gun still went off and hit some other dude at the far end of the bar. He hit the poor sucker right in the chest near his shoulder."

"And was that the end of it?" Nora asked, knowing that it wasn't.

"No, ma'am. Dick yanked his arm away from me and tried to fire a couple times at his original target. Then he walked around the bar and shot the guy right in the ass!"

"Are you sure Mr. Broom had the gun on him? He didn't run out to the car to get it?"

"No, like I said, he pulled it right out of his pants."

"Considering how much you were drinking that night, are you sure you can say that?" Nora pressed.

"Sure as shit, lady. I'll tell you again that he had the gun on him because he was showing it to me earlier in the night."

Nora finally backed off. "So what did you do after he shot Daniel?"

"Are you kidding? I got the hell out of there!" Red clamored. During his cross-examination, Mike reiterated the key point about me having the gun inside the bar for hours prior to the crime. To me that was it; there went the intent.

After being dismissed, Red came by the table. "Sorry, brother. I didn't want to have to testify but the state made me do it."

"I hear you. No worries," I told him and patted him on the back. I guess he didn't realize that his testimony may have saved me from the electric chair. Even if he hadn't, the bottom line was that I wasn't mad at him. I was pissed at myself for being such an idiot. After listening to his testimony and the other witnesses, I began to understand what actually happened and didn't feel too proud about it.

Of course, that wasn't the end of the trial; we still had our own witnesses lined up to testify. We had a bunch of professional people to explain how alcoholism is a disease. One was an RN who pulled out a lot of charts to show the progression of the disease and how it can affect people. Then a counselor from a local rehab shared his experience in the field and identified me as a late-stage alcoholic. Nora tried to undermine his testimony by questioning his credentials. It came out that the only one he had was in interior design. Of course, the bitch made a big deal out of it, humiliating the poor guy as she sarcastically questioned him about how his interior design degree qualified him to know anything about diagnosing alcoholism.

Luckily, she couldn't pull that crap on the clinical psychologist and psychiatrist we subsequently called up. The psychologist reviewed my test results and confirmed that I was indeed an alcoholic and highly irrational, as well. When Nora asked him point-blank if I was legally insane, he said, "No, but he was definitely not thinking clearly and was in a blackout the night of the crime."

Jumping on him, she argued, "How do you know he had a blackout?" When the psychologist told her it was from information he got from me, she snidely responded, "Oh, so he told you he had a blackout."

"Yes, that's correct," the psychologist responded, trying to ignore her sarcasm.

Damn bitch! I couldn't stand her. She totally knew how to twist everything around. I tried to focus on the psychologist's testimony regarding me being an alcoholic, but I knew that their exchange about whether or not I was in a blackout may have undermined our argument.

Nora finally met her match when the psychiatrist, Dr. B., took the stand. He was a cocky guy with a booming voice that made him sound like he knew what he was talking about. His years of experience in the field of psychiatric medicine combined with his pompous attitude gave him an undeniable air of credibility. He did the twisting around this time. In a matter-of-fact tone he explained that I couldn't possibly form the intent to commit first-degree murder.

When Nora asked him if I was insane at the time of the crime, all he said was that he couldn't answer the question. When she asked him again if he thought I was nuts, he said he needed more time with me to make that diagnosis. I wondered why he was leaving that door open—I soon found out why.

His testimony was the last of the day, and as I waited to be transported back to County, Mike paid a visit to the holding cell. "Good news, Dick. Dr. B. said that if you can come up with twenty-five hundred dollars he will see you again."

"Why would I need to see him again? I already saw him," I responded quizzically.

"The doc said that he would be able to testify that you were insane at the time of the crime if he could have another session with you!" Mike said excitedly.

"You mean he would say it if I fork over twenty-five hundred bucks?" I cut to the chase.

"However you want to look at is fine, Dick. Just know that if you can come up with the cash, he could possibly get you off," Mike explained. "Think about it and see what you can do tonight. Let me know what your plan is in the morning."

As soon as I got back to the cell I called Nanny to ask her for the money, but she told me I needed to talk to my mom because she was tapped out. Apparently, there was a huge family feud going on. Big Bob was the only one who came down for the trial because my mom said it was too traumatic for her. Then she and Nanny had a blowout when Bob told her that my lawyer used one of Nanny's letters describing my abusive childhood during his opening argument. Now the two of them were having a battle over whose fault it was that I was nuts.

When I called Mom to ask her for the money, she said she needed to talk to Bob and my brother, Geoff, to see what to do. I called her back later that night and found out that Geoff told her that the doctor's testimony was no guarantee I would get off and that she shouldn't waste any more money on me. I couldn't believe my own brother would screw me over like that! I was convinced that the doctor could sway the jury and even Mike agreed with me. But now, I would never know for sure because I couldn't get the damn money.

The following morning I told Mike that I couldn't come up with the cash. He tried to reassure me that it didn't matter, but I could tell from his reaction that it did. We tried to get on with the day by calling up various character witnesses to testify on my behalf. A bunch of my fraternity brothers talked about how long they knew me, how my drinking patterns changed over the years, how alcohol fueled my violent tendencies, and the difference in my personality between when I was drunk versus when I was sober. When Nora unsuccessfully tried to discount my tendencies for blacking out, she asked them, "Why didn't you tell him to get help for his alcoholism?" One frat brother, George, couldn't give her an answer, while another brother, John, said he was afraid it would hurt our friendship. My fraternity brother Josh became very emotional on the stand as he explained that he tried to help but to no avail. Next up were the ex-wives. Both of them testified about how long they knew me and how my drinking progressed throughout our relationships. Debbie's description of the evolution of my drinking habits clearly matched up to the classic patterns described by the nurse and alcohol counselor. She also brought up a story about how I supposedly raped her when I was drunk and in a blackout. She had confronted me about this before, but I didn't believe her. Sitting in the courtroom listening to her, I began to wonder if it might have really happened. I didn't know because I couldn't remember.

When Nora stepped up to cross-examine Debbie, she used the moment to argue that I always seemed to conveniently forget the things I did wrong. Mike should have objected to her throwing out a statement like that, it wasn't even in the form of a question. But he let it go and I wondered how it would linger in the jurors' minds.

Late that Thursday afternoon, it was my turn to testify on my behalf. Mike felt strongly that the jury needed to hear from me directly and I agreed. He questioned me about what happened on the night of the crime and I explained that the last thing I remember was shooting off my gun into the early night sky. Mike also had me share stories about previous blackouts and my lifelong history of alcohol abuse.

When Nora stepped up, she spent almost all of her time trying to trip me up and discredit me. She made faces, rolled her eyes, and made failed attempts to get me to discount my own testimony. Nothing worked because I was simply telling her the truth.

Mike warned me not to get into a pissing contest with her because the jury would take it as me being aggressive. But after a week of listening to her shit, I couldn't help it. She spent the entire trial giving her closing arguments when she was supposed to just be asking questions. I was sick of her not following the rules. So when she finally finished one of her long, drawn-out statements that was supposed to be a question, I just sat there in silence.

"Well?" she challenged me.

I just looked at her with a blank expression.

"Judge, make him answer the question," she demanded impatiently.

"Oh, I thought you were making another one of your statements. I didn't realize you were actually asking me something so I wasn't really paying attention," I snickered. "Could you repeat the question?"

Nora blew her lid. "Listen you—" then she caught herself and tried to regain her composure. "Your honor, please inform the witness that he needs to answer the question."

Aggravating her even further, the judge told her she needed to pose the question again. Gritting her teeth, she did and I complied. It was the final question of her cross-examination, but I could see her muttering to herself under her breath and I stifled a laugh as I returned to my seat. Mike wasn't happy with me, but I didn't care.

Somebody had to point out that she was constantly testifying to the jury even though she wasn't a witness.

The judge decided that there was no need for any additional character witnesses and informed Mike and Nora that the closing arguments would begin the next morning. I didn't sleep a wink that night. I kept going over and over everything that was said throughout the trial. My life was in the hands of twelve total strangers and I was scared shitless.

Mike and Nora had their game faces on the next day as they gave their closing arguments. Nora just repeated what she was saying all week, but Mike did a brilliant job of connecting all the different testimonies to make his case for me. Before the jury adjourned to deliberate, Mike asked the judge to add manslaughter to the table, in addition to the possible first- and second-degree charges. When the judge agreed to do it, I started to feel more hopeful about things working out in my favor.

The jury was out only two and a half hours and that included the time they spent eating lunch. I was surprised that I was brought back from my holding cell so quickly and could feel myself trembling as I returned to the courtroom. The foreman stood up and announced, "We find the defendant, Richard Broom, guilty of second-degree murder and guilty of second-degree attempted murder."

Chapter Eighteen

IT WOULD BE FORTY LONG DAYS UNTIL MY SENTENCING. All I could do was wait and hope that the judge was lenient and rational and made the sentences concurrent rather than consecutive. Shortly after the trial ended, I met up with Mike to talk about what to expect. I could sense he wasn't that optimistic, but still tried to get him to tell me what I wanted to hear. "It's a no-brainer. The crimes were committed within seconds of each other. How could he possibly make me serve one sentence and then the other?"

"I don't know, Dick. It could go either way."

"I still don't get how they could convict me of second-degree attempted murder. It was obviously an accident."

"Why do you say that?" Mike asked.

"The only reason the guy got shot was because Red yanked my arm. Hell, it was as much his fault as it was mine!" I boomed.

"That may make sense, but it's not how the law sees it. There's a clause that states if you have intent to kill someone and someone else gets killed you are guilty of 'transfer of intent.'"

"But the jury only convicted me of second-degree murder, which means there was no intent," I argued. "How the hell could I have transferred something that I didn't have to begin with?"

"Everything you're saying is completely logical, but it doesn't change a damn thing. The reality is that the jury wasn't trained in the law and sometimes they make mistakes."

"That sucks!

"Yes, it does," Mike agreed. "You should have been a lawyer, Dick."

"I should have done a lot of things," I said as I gazed through the barred windows and thought about how long I might be stuck behind them.

A couple days later I was graced with a visit from Debbie. Somehow she finagled a contact visit where we could sit right across from each other at a table, rather than on opposite sides of a glass partition. Always the drama queen, Debbie made a big deal about being able to pull it off. After all these years, I could tell she was up to something and wasn't in any mood to deal with her antics.

With a very serious look on her face, she began to talk quietly. "I've been putting a lot of thought into what I'm going to say."

Oh, shit. This seems well-rehearsed, I thought to myself.

"I've decided that I am going to wait for you to get out of prison," she said as she took my hand in hers.

When I realized that she meant it, I did one of the kindest things I'd done in a long time: I reminded her of what a complete ass I was. "What? Are you crazy? We just got divorced four months ago!" I laughed in her face.

While shooting her down like that may have seemed mean, I knew it was the only way to get her to change her mind. If I'd been nice, she would have made herself a martyr and played the role to the hilt. So I played the asshole, which obviously came quite naturally to me, and she let go. Somehow we kept the rest of the visit congenial and mutually agreed for me to keep in touch with Erin through letters and an occasional phone call—the same way I was keeping up with Katie. Hopefully, my insanity wouldn't impact their lives too dramatically.

When sentencing day finally arrived, I was called to the stand to testify on my own behalf. Mike kept telling me to show remorse, but I had a hard time connecting emotionally to an incident that I had no honest recollection of—somehow it all still seemed unreal to me. When he realized this, Mike decided the best move would be for me to read my statement and then he would follow up with questions.

So there I was, up on the stand, reading a piece of paper saying that I was sorry, that I didn't know why the crime had happened, and that I wished I had never drunk and gone to the Saloon that day. It all seemed so forced to me, but I did it anyway. Then Mike stepped up and started asking me questions. After all this time, he knew exactly how to get to me. First he dug into my drinking and the mess it made of my life, then he brought up my daughters. He struck a genuine chord in me and I broke down crying on the stand.

Afterward, the judge asked me to stand up to be sentenced. My knees felt weak, but I kept my head up with my eyes on the judge. "Richard Broom, I've decided to give you a life sentence with a concurrent sentence of fifteen years with a three year minimum-maximum sentence." That meant that I would be eligible for parole after doing three years.

The judge continued, "Mr. Broom, you really blew it. You had everything going in your life and you could have done almost anything." I wanted to tell him to kiss my ass, but somehow kept my mouth shut. "Mr. Broom, I strongly urge you to attend Alcoholics Anonymous while you are incarcerated. Your drinking seems to be the main cause of your problems in your life."

He knew how to strike a chord in me as well, except this time he pissed me off. I couldn't help myself. I snapped my right-hand fingers and then pointed at my groin. The judge chose to ignore my obscene gesture and ended the proceedings.

I was then escorted back to my holding cell where I changed my clothes and left my suit and dress boots for Mike to pick up from the County guards. By the time he came to pick them up, they had disappeared. I guess the pigs were exactly what I thought they were: thieves with a badge.

Back in my jail cell, I was consumed with hate and what I thought was justified anger for everyone involved in the justice system. The next day I found a local paper featuring a story about my case. A woman reporter who had originally called me a monster at the beginning of my trial now called me a poor, sick man. What the hell did she know?

Chapter Nineteen

THREE DAYS LATER I WAS SHACKLED AND STUFFED into a van with two-by-ten wooden seats. The van was owned by a company called Inmate Transit and was hired by the state to move prisoners from county jails in south Florida to Lake Butler Reception and Medical Center. In 1983, all prisoners in the state of Florida were sent there first. There it was decided to which permanent party prison all new inductees would be sent.

The drive was brutal. They squeezed twenty prisoners into a van that was made to fit fourteen passengers at most. I was miserable the entire ride, sweating my balls off, chained to the bench like an animal. When the bus stopped off at company headquarters for lunch, a nasty woman begrudgingly handed each of us a baloney sandwich. We remained shackled as we ate, so I had to bend down to my waist to take each bite.

Of course, I knew that this wasn't punishment dealt out by the system, but capitalism at its worst. Greed was rearing its ugly head, and these bastards were getting the most bang for their buck. As the ride went on, my blood began to boil and I decided that I was going to take down the owners of this company as soon as I got out. I made a mental note to add these pigs to my list, right along with the judge, the lying detectives, and Nora, of course. Fantasizing about my revenge made the rest of the ride more bearable.

Normally it would take four and a half hours to complete the trip, but it took us almost ten hours to get there that day. When we finally arrived at Lake Butler in the early evening, I was as glad to get out of that van as I had been to get out of County Jail after 359 days. Once inside the gates, the chains came off and I could finally stretch out to ease the pain in my lower back. We were then herded to where the uniforms and bedding were handed out. It was a big day: we received our official prison numbers, which we had to memorize and recite on command for any corrections officer. My new name became 090221. I wasn't cool enough to get a letter, just a number; the letters were reserved for inmates who had a history of incarceration. The As were guys in for the second time, Bs for the third time, and so on.

We were then marched over to the building we would be calling home for the next few weeks. The inside seemed like an open dorm. I had pictured two-man cells with slamming steel doors, but I was brought to a large room with lots of bunks in it instead. According to some of the letter-sporting cons, you only went into one of those smaller cells if you were a problem inmate.

I was quickly learning that the letter men were the go-to guys when you were looking to figure out how things ran around the joint. They were the ones who gave me the heads up on which guards to watch out for. There was D-Wing Tim, who found particular pleasure in disciplining inmates who stepped out of line. He would take them to solitary, cuff them, and beat them bloody. You didn't fuck with D-Wing Tim; he was one bad country boy. Then there was, Charlie, a black lieutenant who thought he was white. As a child, he was adopted by one of the white families who ran the northern part of the state's prisons and he hated all the inmates. Apparently, many black inmates over the years made the mistake of calling Charlie "brother." He would typically respond by saying, "I ain't your brother!" and then kick their ass. He was someone you didn't mess with either. He was a bad man who thought nothing of beating inmates down. There were other legends in this strange society, as well. The common thread among them was that they viewed the inmates as pieces of shit and made sure we knew it.

On my third day, I was in the chow hall when I ran into my old pal from County, Bob the Polack. He had copped a plea of three years for his strong-armed robbery charge, and apparently Lake Butler was his permanent party gig. He was slogging out food on the lunch line when I ran into him.

"Yo, Bobby! How you doing, you bastard!" I greeted him boisterously.

"Shush, Dick! Not here, not now," he whispered with a scared look on his face. Apparently, this place had gotten to him. Covering his mouth so no one could see his lips were moving, "I can't talk to you. If I get caught I'll get my ass kicked."

Bob caught up with me on the sly later on and explained. "This place gets away with a lot of shit, Dick. They are fucking brutal around here. I just can't make any waves."

"What the hell are you talking about, man? All I did was say hello!" I wasn't taking him seriously.

"Us permanent party guys aren't supposed to be talking to people being classified here, like you," he explained, nervously looking around.

"I get it. Sorry. The last thing I want to do is to get you into trouble," I said and then shook his hand. "Good luck, brother." With that, I left him alone with his fear.

Not long after that, I finally met up with a man they called my "classification officer." He had me take a bunch of aptitude tests and then told me that with my high IQ, I would probably get a decent job while in prison, maybe something in the law library. He then asked me, "So how long do you think you'll spend on the inside before getting paroled?"

"Probably ten years or so," I guessed.

He laughed, which I thought was odd because I was as serious as a heart attack. "No, no, no," he continued to chuckle. "You probably won't do more than seven years and maybe as little as five if you can keep a good prison record. For your crime, a first-time offense, the parole guidelines state that you should do eighty to one hundred months—that is, six years and eight months to eight years and four months."

I didn't believe him, but went along with it. I figured he was conning me so I wouldn't cause them too much trouble. I had no plans to cause any problems unless I was cornered and forced to fight.

He continued. "If you keep DR-free or only get a couple DRs, you won't spend more than seven years in prison."

"Okay, but what's a DR?"

"That's short for Disciplinary Report—something the corrections officers write up if you break the rules. Everyone has a file and everything you do, good or bad, goes into that file. For a lesser offense, you only get a CC or Corrective Consultation. But if you get three CCs within a six-month period, it counts as a DR. If you get too many DRs, your parole would probably be denied until you showed improvement."

"Got it," I nodded.

"Alright, now I see here that you've been classified to go to either Glades Correctional Institute in Western Palm Beach County, Union Correctional Institute, a.k.a. Raiford, or Florida State Prison in Starke. Which one of these do you want to go to?"

After thinking about it for less than five seconds, I blurted out, "I don't want to go to Glades." The only reason I said that was because

I figured that if I told them I didn't want to go there, that's where they would send me.

Unfortunately, I was mistaken. I was shipped off to Raiford, also known as the Rock. The place was infamous. I had heard a lot about it in County. Everyone talked about it as if it was the worst place in the world. According to the horror stories, it was an extremely violent place. There was a constant struggle between the guards and inmates for control of the prison, and the inmates usually had the upper hand. After seeing how Lake Butler was run, it was hard to believe that inmates could rule the roost anywhere, but I soon found out that it was true.

Located in a small town in north Florida, about forty-five miles west of Jacksonville, Raiford was the oldest prison in the state. When you first pull up to the front of the main housing unit, it looks almost like a typical main street in Middle America. There's a cozy restaurant, tiny chapel, friendly-looking local hospital, and several other buildings with that small-town charm—that is, of course, if you have your back to the main housing unit. The prison looked like a medieval fort. To enter it you had to walk through a giant, ominous-looking arch.

Upon our arrival, we were greeted by a gauntlet of cons selling their wares. It was reminiscent of a Middle Eastern open market. They were selling pot, buck, shanks—one guy even claimed he had a sword for sale. All of this was done right in front of the guards. Apparently, the inmates really did run the prison on the inside, and from the looks of the scene, I wasn't sure if that was a good thing. Our bunks were only eighteen inches apart, side-by-side in an open room. There was no doubt that the living conditions violated all sorts of codes.

I only lived like that for about five days, but on my second night I listened to a man being raped. A young newbie went into the showers and was followed by five booty bandits.

"Stop! Stop! Leave me alone!" I heard the guy whining from the shower. "Please, stop!"

I jumped up to help him when Frank, an old con from Louisiana, stopped me. "Mind your own business, son."

Having spent a couple five-to-ten year stints in other prisons, I listened to him. He obviously knew the score when it came to this society's do's and don'ts. "If he stops begging and starts fighting, we'll both go help him. But if he won't fight for his own ass, why should we? You don't want to wind up getting shanked or end up in solitary do you?"

So while the white boy got raped four or five times, I did nothing except learn a lesson of survival: when in prison, never try to help those who won't try to help themselves. I didn't want to get into the middle of a race war, especially when the blacks made up 65 percent of the prison's population. When I met with my classification officer, Mr. Marin, he told me I was moving into the A wing of the main housing unit and would work in the chow hall slinging slop and cleaning up. "That's a real wise decision on your part, considering that I'm one of the only inmates out of twenty-five hundred with a college degree," I grumbled.

Ignoring my attitude, Mr. Marin explained, "In here, you have to work your way up to the better jobs. The best way for you to get a job best suited for your talents is to get to know the other inmates in those positions. For example, if you want to work in the school as a teacher's assistant, you need to know the inmates who work there. They would be the ones to suggest to their bosses that you get to work there. And what better place to meet all these people than in the chow hall?"

So there I was, working in the dining room and living large on the A-floor. My cell was big, but it had six bunks in it. Two of the beds were in the front of the cell, below the barred window opening, with the cell door between them. The two sets of bunks were against the sidewalls with the sink and toilet bowl against the back wall. The cell was about fifteen feet wide and ten feet deep. There was a lot of space in the middle of the cell and a fold-up table with a couple of folding chairs. I stayed on the upper bunk on the right side of the cell. It was an upgrade from the west unit.

My cell pals were all white except for a short, non-English speaking Mexican named José. He never said anything to anyone, he just sat and stared—and always went to bed early. One night, I woke up at about 3:00 AM to witness the little Mexican performing some kind of ritual. He had candles lit all over the floor and was pacing around the cell, quietly going through some gyrations. I noticed that my cell mate Tex was awake and also eyeballing the crazy Mexican. This was obviously some kind of religious thing and neither Tex nor I liked the idea of Shorty prancing around the cell during the middle of the night. Tex finally yelled at José to cut the shit and I chimed in. He immediately blew out the candles and jumped back into bed.

Out of morbid curiosity, I followed Jose to the yard the next day. I wanted to see how he spent his day and it wasn't long before I was thrust into complete culture shock. There he was, crawling around the ground along the base of a wall, using his clawlike fingernails to capture and eat bugs he dug up from the dirt. I immediately shared this with Tex and we took off to talk to another Central American he knew on the compound.

"He's trying to become an animal," explained Santos, Tex's compadre. "It's some kind of religion, you know, where you worship nature and stuff. The little guy must be trying to transform himself into a gopher or a sloth."

Tex and I burst out laughing.

"Oh, yeah, you guys might want to check his mattress, man," added Santos.

"Why?" Tex grinned.

"He might be burying feces inside of it," Santos replied. He was completely serious.

Tex and I took off for our cell right away and sure enough, the mattress was torn open and there was shit and other crap stuffed inside it. We immediately dumped the mattress under the stairwell, declaring that the gopher no longer resided in our cell.

A sergeant in the control booth called Tex and me in, along with the other two guys from our cell. "Who the hell do you think you are?" he yelled. "You can't just move another inmate!"

We tried to explain about the bug eating, the middle-of-the-night candle opera, and the feces-stuffed mattress, but the sergeant wouldn't listen. Finally, we warned him, "The gopher is not living with us anymore! And if you insist on him staying there, we are not responsible for the accidental death that will happen in our cell!"

"Fine, he's out," the sergeant gave in and moved José to practice his belief system in someone else's cell. Evidently, rational reasoning held little sway in Raiford. The only language anyone seemed to listen to was violence.

It was a way of life there and you were a fool not to realize that. Even if you wanted to keep out of it, sometimes you had no choice. I was drawn into it working in the chow hall when a Mandingo warrior came onto my line demanding more stew.

"Don't do it," growled the guard behind me.

"Listen white boy, gimme some more of that damn stew!" the warrior roared.

"Don't you dare give him anything," ordered the guard.

Stuck in the middle, I wasn't sure what to do. Before I could make a move, the six-feet, four-inch muscular warrior wailed his tray across my face. I reacted by leaning over the steam table to whop him over the head with a ladle. The guards immediately halted the altercation, but I knew it wouldn't be the end of it.

I had to finish the confrontation, otherwise I would be looking over my shoulder until Mandingo did. That was the law of this twisted society. If you showed fear, you would become someone's prey. So that evening after supper I went looking for the warrior on his wing, which happened to be all black. I stormed in, acting as if I belonged there, until I found the badass. His upper body was tightly muscled but his legs were spindly, even smaller than my arms. To me that meant that he only worked out on his upper body, so he was all show. Catching him off guard, I pounded him at least ten times—he never even landed a punch. When he was down on the ground in front of his cell, I asked him, "Is that it?"

"Yes," he whimpered pathetically. I walked out with an even bigger attitude. All the brothers on the wing thought I was a crazy white boy and no one bothered me for a while.

After all this nonsense, I needed a drink, but it wasn't like I could walk into a bar and order one. Or was it? During the first couple days at the Rock I noticed a guy named Coco staggering across the compound. I figured he'd be able to show me where I could find some buck. It turned out it was much easier to get in Raiford. You didn't have to make it yourself; it was sold all over the prison. There were a bunch of watering holes where you could choose from a variety of styles: applejack, prune, raisin, or orange-aid. Of course, it all still tasted like flavored gasoline—but at least it got you drunk.

The first day Coco took me around, I caught a good buzz. I felt as if I was back in high school again, sneaking around and getting loaded when the timing was right. As soon as I sobered up, I looked forward to my next chance to get drunk.

In order to pay for the buck, I started selling my blood. Every other Tuesday I would give blood for $10, and then go directly to one of the winemakers. They didn't want you drinking near where the wine was kept, but they also didn't want you dragging a gallon jug around with you either. So you would drink it as fast as you could before anyone could catch you.

On September 10, 1983, I followed my typical routine. After giving blood, then putting down a fifth of buck, I staggered back to serve supper. The next thing I knew it was the following morning. I had my first prison blackout and it must have lasted about sixteen hours.

When I went to work that afternoon, Harold, the only other white guy working in the chow hall, came up to me with a nervous look on his face. "I don't know what you were thinking, man. You have to watch yourself," he warned me.

"What the hell are you talking about?" I asked

"You need to chill out," said Harold in a low voice. "You got completely out of hand last night!"

"What happened?" I was afraid of what he was going to say.

"You don't remember? That figures! Someone pissed you off and you grabbed a mop handle, started going off on all the brothers, and then chased a bunch of them down. I thought you were going to kill them!"

"You're full of shit!" I challenged him. "If I had done what you said, I'd be locked up!"

"Homeboy, the guards just locked you in and let you go after them!" Harold exclaimed. "They didn't give a shit. As far as they were concerned either there would be a couple of dead niggers or one dead Yankee—and either way was alright with them!"

"I gotta stop this shit," I said as much to myself as to Harold. "I guess I gotta go to that twelve-step shit."

And it was then that I had what some call my "moment of clarity." I finally acknowledged that the drinking had to stop. Without realizing it, I made the first step in the Twelve-Step program: I admitted that I was powerless over alcohol. It was time to face the fact that I had tried to control my drinking for years, but it always controlled me. No matter what I did, I would inevitably end up falling-down drunk or close to it. I even reached the point where making myself unconscious was the only way to be happy. There had to be something more.

That night I filled out a request form asking my classification officer to allow me to attend a Twelve-Step meeting held every other Sunday in the visiting park. It was a decision that would change my life.

Chapter Twenty

AFTER PUTTING IN MY REQUEST FOR A PASS TO A Twelve-Step meeting, I ended up being given a pass to the chapel instead. I was summoned by the chaplain, so even though I didn't want to go, I had to. I figured he was probably trying to turn me into some kind of born-again, but I didn't believe in God and there was nothing he was going to say to change that. Sure, I sent out some foxhole prayers from the county jail to get me out of trouble, but as far as I was concerned, none of them were answered. I'd come to the conclusion that if, somehow, there actually was a God, I was his court jester put on earth to entertain him and his minions.

When I arrived at the chapel, a tall skinny man who looked like he came straight out of the movie *Deliverance* greeted me at the door. "Hello, Richard. I am Reverend Walton, the head chaplain here."

"Uh, hello," I said, not sure why I was even there.

"I was hoping we could begin by exploring your spiritual journey thus far," he said. "Were you raised in any particular religious persuasion?"

"Yep, my parents dragged me to a Presbyterian church as a kid. But when the minister would preach his fire and brimstone sermons, he'd look right at me and say that I was going to hell if I broke any of the commandments. By the time I was eight I'd already broken the 'Thou shall not steal' commandment, so I figured I was already screwed. I figured I might as well just do what I wanted to do if I was headed for the hellfires anyway."

"What about now? Have you found your way back to the Lord?" he pressed.

"I don't practice anything now," I answered. Trying to be honest, I told him point blank, "Listen, I don't believe in God. Even if there was one, I wouldn't want to worship him if he was into punishing everyone. Hell, I don't even know why I'm here."

"I understand you asked to attend a Twelve-Step meeting?" he asked as if he didn't know the answer.

"Yes, I did. I wanted to see what it was all about. I don't want to drink anymore." I had to be careful. I didn't want him to know that I was drinking buck several times a week.

"Well, you know those twelve-step programs are based on spiritual fundamentals. You don't even need to go to those meetings to stay sober. You can get sober by simply giving your life to Jesus."

Up until then, I didn't know that the twelve-step program was a spiritual program, which to me meant it was religious. I was disappointed because I'd given up on religion a long time ago. Then I figured out that the reverend was probably just lying to get me join his flock.

"I still think I want to give the program a shot," I said, trying to brush him off.

Realizing he might be losing a sale, he kicked his pitch into high gear. "I can help you stay sober right here. You don't need those meetings." Suddenly his Florida backwoods accent came out, "Jeeesus will help you to beat your demons!"

I started to get pissed off. "Listen, I'm not interested in God, Jesus, or this chapel."

That didn't phase the preacher one bit. He raised his arms up to the sky and started shouting, "I know you are ready to put Jeee-sus into your life. I can feel it! Get on your knees right now and let Jeee-sus come into your life!"

"I don't think so," I said, but he ignored me.

Warmed up, he boomed, "I know you are ready. I can see it in your eyes. Get on your knees!"

"Why don't you get on your knees and put something in your life!" I hollered back.

Shocked, the preacher demanded that I get out of his chapel.

"That's what I've been trying to do all along!" I snarled as I walked out the doors.

When I got back to my cell I started worrying that maybe he was telling the truth about the Twelve-Step program being religious. Even though I didn't think it would work for me, I was at the point where I was willing to give it 100 percent. But if it was religious, I just couldn't handle it and that meant I was done. I would wind up like Coco, a hopeless alcoholic spending the rest of his life in prison. I didn't want to end up that way, so I decided to follow up on getting my pass to a meeting so I could at least find out what it was all about.

A few days later, I got another pass, but again it wasn't for the meeting. This time it was to go see a psychologist. After waiting outside his office for almost an hour, he opened his door and greeted me like we were old chums. This, of course, immediately set off alarm bells.

As soon as I was seated in his office, he jumped right in. "I see that you asked to attend a Twelve-Step meeting, is that right?"

I couldn't understand why the hell all these people kept asking me questions that they already knew the answers to. "Yes, that's right," I answered.

Then just like Reverend Righteous, Dr. Mindgames said, "You don't need to go to a meeting. I can help you get and stay sober as long as we can form a bond of trust between us."

What the hell am I doing here and what is this fool talking about? I thought to myself.

"In fact," he continued, "if we can establish this trust between each other, I can actually cure you of this disease."

I didn't know anything about alcoholism, drug addiction, or Twelve-Step programs, but somehow that didn't sound kosher to me. I remembered Nanny telling me that my biological father had walked all the way to Poughkeepsie to find a cure for his alcoholism and that even the state's mental institution couldn't help him. She also said that maybe AA might have been able to.

So there I was, listening to this man who had to be a complete loser if he was working for the prison system, and he was trying to convince me that he could cure me of my pathological drinking habit. Although I saw right through him, I decided to see where he was going with this.

"So you are ready to form this bond of trust with me?" he asked.

"Yes," I lied.

"Good," he smiled. Then after hesitating for about two seconds, he asked me, "Who stabbed the guy on A wing last night, five cells down from you?"

There it was, the real reason why he wanted to form that "bond of trust."

"I don't know," I answered. It was the truth.

Dr. Mindgames didn't like my answer. "See, we can't start our relationship without you being honest with me."

"I am being honest with you," I sighed. "I didn't even know that anyone was stabbed last night, much less who did it."

"Ohhh, no . . . this isn't going to work if you won't tell me the truth. You see, I can't cure you if you're not honest with me."

That was it. I wasn't going to sit there and have some guy who was trying to take advantage of the fact that I'm looking for help call me a liar. I leaned over and got right in his face. "I don't care whether you believe me or not. I'm telling the truth. All I want is to go to a goddamn meeting. I didn't ask to see you and I wouldn't trust you if you were the last man on earth!"

"I see right through you," I continued to go off. "All you want is some snitch so you can make yourself look good in front of the prison administration!"

Dr. Mindgames didn't say anything for a few minutes; he just turned a bright shade of red. Finally, he snapped back, "Do you know what you are? You're a sociopath with a mafia mentality!"

"Thank you!" I laughed.

"Get out of my office," yelled Dr. Mindgames.

As I left the office, I came to the conclusion that I really couldn't trust anyone. I couldn't trust my family, certainly not my lying mother, abusive stepfather, or greedy brother. I couldn't trust either of my crazy ex-wives or even crazier girlfriends. I certainly couldn't trust any of the cons in here, and I would be completely nuts to trust the guards, classification officers, preachers, or even the therapists.

I was on my own, which meant that I was completely fucked.

Chapter Twenty-One

A FEW DAYS LATER A GUARD SHOWED UP AT MY CELL. "Broom, got something for you," he called. He handed me a piece of paper. It was a pass to the next Twelve-Step meeting scheduled for Sunday, which was only three days away. Considering everything the prison authorities did to try to prevent me from going, I figured there must be something magical about it. For the first time in months, I grinned.

When the big day finally came, an announcement was made over the loudspeaker. "All those scheduled to go to the Twelve-Step meeting today, be ready in five minutes." Exactly five minutes later, my cell door opened. I stepped out and trotted through the corridor, ignoring the jeers of the inmates calling me a wimp and a drunken fool, among other things. About a hundred of us were escorted over to a pavilion in the visiting park where there were another two hundred inmates waiting to be checked in. As I listened to the chatter of the crowd, it became apparent that many of the men were there because their classification officers ordered them to go. I, on the other hand, was anxious to get inside to find out what this was all about.

Once my name was checked off the list, I entered the pavilion and found my way to a seat at one of the picnic tables in the back where a pack of the Aryan brothers were. Gazing around the room, I took in the scene. Just like the rest of the prison, each racial group seemed to stick to its own. In the front of the room, five inmates were sitting on a stage with a microphone. Hanging from beams above them were two banners: one said "Twelve Steps" and the other said "Twelve Traditions." Each one had twelve sentences under them and I immediately felt sick to my stomach as I began to read them. The word "God" was written at least a half dozen times. *Damn!* I thought to myself. *Reverend Righteous wasn't lying. They push this God crap, too.* I was still determined to give it a shot and decided that I would skip steps two, three, six, seven, and eleven. After further review, I also decided that I wasn't going to have anything to do with the first parts of steps five or twelve, either.

The guards led in nine civilians, five men and four women. I'd heard about volunteers bringing meetings to the prisons and was impressed when I found out that they drove from fifty miles away and spent four hours of their own time to reach out to a bunch of losers like us. I was also delighted to see some good-looking women for the first time in a while. Waiting for the meeting to start, one of the Aryan brothers questioned why the volunteers were there. Apparently, he was as new to this as I was.

"They get paid to be here," claimed one con at the table.

"It's because they have legal problems and this is their community service," suggested another bonehead.

"No way, man. The chicks come here because they are looking for a real man and all the real men are in prison!" boasted one of the bikers at the end of the table.

"That's why the men are here, too. They are all looking for a real man!" his buddy quipped and the table erupted in hearty laughter.

Eventually, things quieted down when the actual meeting began with everyone reciting the Serenity Prayer. Next up was an inmate reading "How It Works," a spiel explaining the Twelve Steps. Other inmates followed him, reviewing the Twelve Traditions and reading a preamble describing the program.

After all that, some tall black inmate named George, who seemed to be the head honcho, got up and started preaching about leaving your twelve steps on the fence when you leave prison. I guess he was talking to some of the guys who were getting out soon. Even though he was spewing all this God propaganda, I was still paying attention and listened even closer when he presented one of the women volunteers named Kay.

After introducing herself as an alcoholic, she spoke for ten minutes about how frustrated and even furious she would get with herself when she couldn't keep herself from drinking. She said she drank against her will and eventually found herself feeling helpless and hopeless. When she began going to the Twelve-Step program and met other people with the same struggle who had stayed sober for years, she found hope for herself.

Kay's story struck a chord. As I listened to her, I came to the realization that maybe I wasn't alone. There were other people who felt trapped by alcohol, who experienced the anger and disappointment of being unable to break the cycle of drinking. As additional speakers got up to share their struggles, I began to think that I might be able to stay sober like them—at least for a while. Hell, I hadn't had a drink since my blackout two weeks ago—that was a good start! I decided I would try to stay sober at least for that day and maybe even till the next meeting—two weeks away. I didn't think I'd be able to stop drinking for good. Trapped in this twisted place, there were going to be times when I would need to get loaded to deal with the madness, but for now I wanted to stay sober—at least until the next meeting.

When the meeting came to an end, everyone got into a huge circle, held hands, and said the Lord's Prayer. I didn't want to hold hands with any of the sick bastards there, nor did I want to recite the prayer. I stepped to the outside of the circle and waited for the mumbo-jumbo to be over.

Later on, back in my cell, I thought about the meeting and decided that it did make me feel better, despite all the religious shtick. It was encouraging to hear people who actually made some sense. I was already looking forward to going back in two weeks.

Wanting to give the whole sobriety thing my best shot, I decided it was time to keep busy with positive things. So I signed up for a program called Substance Abuse: Phase 1, and put in a request to participate in Go-Lab, an eight-day, eight-hour-a-day behavioral modification program. Fellow inmates ran both programs, and I wondered what a bunch of lowlifes could teach me, but I decided to see what they had to offer. Even if the programs couldn't keep me sober, signing up for them would make me look good to the parole commission and get me out of working in the chow hall for a while.

Two weeks later, I still hadn't heard back on either program, but I hadn't had a drink either. When I went to my next meeting, I sat a bit further up so I could hear more from the volunteers. Only one of the young hotties was there, along with Kay and four other guys. Again inmates got up and read off laminated papers, and the older black guy George preached about leaving AA at the gate. By sitting closer this time, I noticed that George was sucking on a mouthful of breath mints, and he started to sway back and forth. There was no denying that he was loaded. I couldn't believe that he was up there running off at the mouth, and he couldn't even stay sober once every two weeks.

Ignoring his hypocrisy, I tried to get something out of the stories shared by other inmates. It paid off when I learned how I could say no to having a drink. I had been approached several times to purchase some liquid libation since I'd stopped drinking, and I'd struggled with turning it down. When I told the winemakers that I didn't have any money, they would still push it on me, telling me I could pay for it later. According to the other inmates, simply invoking the phrase "twelve step" could get them off my back. Of course, it would be hard to do. I really did want to slip into oblivion, and in most cases the winemakers would respond by saying, "Let me know when you get over that shit." I decided to try the twelve-step phrase the next time I was facing temptation.

Just like two weeks ago, the meeting wrapped up with the Lord's Prayer and with me waiting on the outside of the circle. But this time I didn't just leave. I worked my way up to the front of the pavilion to introduce myself to Bill, one of the guys from Go-Lab.

"Uh, hi. I'm Richard Broom," I said awkwardly. "I hear you guys are connected with Go-Lab. I just put in my request to get into the program."

"Okay, great! We'll look for it," Bill replied, distracted by someone else trying to get his attention

"Yeah, it's under Broom, Richard Broom. That's easy to remember, right?" I said as he began to walk away.

"Sure, Richard," he waved. "We'll keep an eye out for it." I had no doubt that he would forget to look.

Still eager to keep making progress, I set out to find a copy of the *Big Book* that everyone kept talking about during the meetings. I headed into the prison library on the hunt for it. I started out in the nonfiction section, but because I didn't know the name of the author, I looked at every single book in the section. With no luck there, I moved on to the fiction section and it wasn't there either. I finally found it buried in the reference section, covered in dust next to an incomplete encyclopedia. Since it looked like no one else had used it in a long time, I decided that it was okay to smuggle it back to my cell.

I read the *Big Book* in two days. The first time I read it, I related to some parts of it. The second time I read it, I got even more out of it. For the next several months I'd read it over and over again—and each time I would find a few more things that applied to me.

By my third meeting, I felt like I was taking the program seriously. I wasn't drinking and hadn't since my last meeting. Hell, I was so serious that I stole the *Big Book!* Trying to get even more out of the meeting, I decided to sit right up front, seventy-five feet closer than I was during my first meeting. It seemed like a whole different world up there. No one was making wisecracks; everyone seemed more mature. As I listened to people sharing their stories, I recognized that they were talking about a lot of the same themes that were covered in my book, the *Big Book*.

As I sat there congratulating myself for coming so far with the program, I was thrust even further into it when George handed me a copy of "How It Works" and told me he'd like me to read it later on in the meeting. My hands trembling, I kept reading it over and over to myself before he called me up. When George introduced me, I tried to hide the fact that my legs were shaking. The last thing I wanted was for 300 convicts to sense my fear.

Taking a deep breath, I began to read: *"Rarely have we seen a person fail who has thoroughly followed our path. Those who do not recover are people who cannot or will not completely give themselves to this simple program, usually men and women who are constitutionally incapable of being honest with themselves."* I continued reading all four pages. Minutes later, when I was done, I had no idea what I'd read or any recollection of hearing myself read it. I simply slipped back into my seat and let out a heavy sigh of relief. Still, I felt that compared to all the risks I'd taken in my past, none took more courage than that one.

Chapter Twenty-Two

WITHIN TWO WEEKS I FOUND MYSELF SITTING IN A clean, air-conditioned classroom, starting my first day of Go-Lab. It felt like an oasis from the brutal and chaotic culture that pervaded every other inch of Raiford. The classroom was located in the South West Unit, a new building that was considered the safest place in the Rock. Only people who completed the Go-Lab program were able to live there, and there was a strict code of conduct to follow. If you committed a violent crime while living there you had to move out. Sick of living in fear and constantly watching my back, I made a vow to myself that I would do whatever it took to be transferred into the unit. The Twelve-Step meetings had already given me a sense of hope, and I was curious how Go-Lab, which stood for "Growth Orientation Laboratory, could free me from my addiction. I soon found out that my drinking wasn't my only problem.

When the session began, we were greeted by a colorful crew of inmates who were serving as our instructors. The guy in charge, Jerry, was a slick street gangster from Chicago who used to have a problem with heroin and was locked up for manslaughter. Tom was a fairly cool guy from Pompano, Florida, who had a second-degree murder charge, plus an armed robbery conviction. Bill, the typist, who also ran a couple groups, was in for kidnapping, attempted murder, and bunch of other charges that came from a crazy ride through Tampa. Bob said he was in for burglary but was really in for rape, and Gerald was an airline pilot who had murdered his wife's boyfriend. Yup, these were the guys who were going to teach me how to behave well and play nicely with others.

My skepticism quickly faded once Jerry began his introductory presentation to twenty of us thugs. He was enthusiastic, articulate, and spoke confidently to us for over thirty minutes. Maybe he wasn't such a loser after all.

As the week progressed I began to reevaluate my snap judgment of the group leaders. The lectures and group discussions they led were humorous and educational, and they captured the attention of most of the guys in our group. Their honesty and directness gave them a credibility that someone like Dr. Mindgames could never have. They helped me begin to examine why I thought the way I did. The group leaders began by explaining how our life experiences are stored as mental images that become our frame of reference for how we view the world. We then look at all subsequent experiences through that frame of reference and decide how to react accordingly.

While I'd spent all those months in County reflecting on my life experiences, it took Go-Lab for me to understand how my experiences growing up impacted my choices later in life; by the time I was a toddler, for example, I was punching geese because Bob had already taught me that if you don't like what someone is doing, hit him. As life went on, I lost all sense of right and wrong. I would hit someone over the head with a case of beer if he cut me on line, just to protect my ego. But my experiences couldn't be used as excuses either.

Through classes on choices and freedom, I began to recognize that it was up to me to take control and make the right decisions.

Maybe I did learn to strike out from my parents, but I could have let it go and moved on with my life. I didn't have to wallow in it and use it as an excuse to get messed up all the time and completely fuck up my life. I was also the one responsible for allowing alcohol to control my life. It was up to me to find the worthwhile person I'd spent years burying underneath ego, self-centeredness, and alcohol. The good news was that I could make that change.

By the end of the week's session I was exhausted and sad that it was over. When Jerry informed us that there was another five-day program called Advanced Go-Lab, I immediately signed up for it. It wasn't scheduled to start for another four months; I wished that it would start next week. I didn't want to return to the prison jungle. I was finally beginning to figure out why I was me, and I was ready to make some real changes in my life. It was the only way I'd ever have a decent life if I ever made it out of prison.

I also knew that I couldn't change too much while I was still in the joint if I wanted to survive inside. If I got too soft, I'd become a target. I needed to stay tough. I was still stuck in one of the most violent prisons in the country. There were about fourteen murders a year there and another three hundred or so serious assaults. No matter who you were in Raiford, you had to look over your shoulder every ten steps or so to see who was behind you. So I did my best to walk the line, going to Twelve-Step meetings in order to grow as a person, but maintaining my badass attitude when I worked in the chow hall.

Somehow fate shined down on me when I got my pass to escape to Advanced Go-Lab. It was much sooner than expected and I didn't ask why. I was just relieved to get out of the chow hall and back to the South West Unit, away from 2T.

During Advanced Go-Lab I began to see the parallels with what we talked about in our Twelve-Step meetings. In meetings we'd talk about the importance of addressing our emotional, physical, and spiritual needs. Go-Lab introduced us to the Total Man concept, which addresses the importance of meeting those three needs, but also our intellectual and social needs.

The program's sessions made me explore how I could find greater balance in my life by working on areas where I was weakest and maintaining those where I was most proficient. During my subsequent years in prison, I applied this concept by reading more, getting involved in team sports again, and taking other steps to make sure I was working on all five aspects of my being. We also had lectures on accomplishments, fulfillment, expectations, and recognition, as well as internal and external motivators. By the end of the five days, I felt fulfilled and, again, disappointed that it was over.

As I was getting ready to leave, Jerry, Tom, and Gerald pulled me aside and asked me if I wanted to work there as an instructor. I was ecstatic, but terrified at the same time. Of course, it would get me out of the chow hall and 2T. I'd be able to live in the unit, and best of all, I'd be immersed in a completely positive atmosphere. The only drawback was my own self-doubt. How could I possibly learn close to one hundred lectures? Would I really be able to get up and speak for hours in front of other inmates? Sick of letting my fear run my life, I said yes.

Two weeks later I started working in Go-Lab and living in the new unit. My first step was kicking off the sessions with a morning rap. All I had to do was take a word like "trust," "responsibility," "love," "anger," or "respect," and talk about it for five minutes. Then I would get everyone else in the group to talk about it. The first morning I was supposed to do it, I was paralyzed with fear—literally. I was sitting in the office, preparing to go in and start the session, but couldn't move. I was so afraid of failure, so consumed with my own ego again, that I froze up and Gerald had to run the group.

The other leaders tried to be supportive of me, but told me that I absolutely had to do it the next morning. I didn't sleep a wink that night; I just tossed and turned, becoming more and more anxious about screwing up. Ironically, by the time the morning came around I was so worn out that I didn't have the energy to be scared anymore. I told myself to act as if I knew what I was doing, and I charged into the classroom and started talking. As soon as I got going, I realized that it wasn't that big a deal.

Within a few months I was doing most of the lectures and felt confident running all of them. Years ago, I would have needed three or four shots to get up to introduce a wedding party, and now I was able to talk for hours to groups of hardened criminals. I was evolving from a man consumed with self-doubt and fear to one with a sense of self-esteem. I began to really believe that what I was teaching could change a person's life. I was glad to go to work every morning and looked forward to learning something from others and about myself every day. Even though I was locked up and wasn't sure if I would ever get out, I finally felt like I was accomplishing something worthwhile.

A few months into working at Go-Lab, I called Mom and Big Bob. They were on the line at the same time, each one on a different phone, and both of them were giving me shit. Cutting them off, I told them, "You know what? I forgive you two."

It got real quiet. After a minute of silence, I said, "Okay. I'll talk to you in a month," then hung up the phone. They never called me a piece of crap again.

Chapter Twenty-Three

AS THE WEEKS WENT BY, I BEGAN TO FEEL AS IF A huge weight had been lifted off my shoulders. Somehow, I wasn't carrying around all that anger toward Mom and Big Bob anymore, plus I hadn't had a drink in months. People were still offering me buck, vodka, and other homemade spirits, but I found the strength to say no. I can't deny that I still longed for that carefree feeling booze would give me. But before I could take a swill, I would force myself to remember gagging down drinks while vomiting and defecating at the same time. I would also think about the shame and guilt I felt when I saw the look on my daughter Katie's face after I missed picking her up because of a bender. The memory of the sadness and confusion in her eyes haunted me, and the mere thought of it was all it took for me to tell the other cons, "No, thanks. I'm still going to that twelve-step shit."

Between the meetings and Go-Lab, I tried to find shelter from the vices and violence that pervaded the rest of the prison. While I wanted to start a new life, I was still sentenced to spend it in a madhouse. The harsh reality was that being a part of Go-Lab didn't automatically excuse us from the brutality of Raiford. I was reminded of this over and over as I witnessed one incident after another where guys who made it through the program still fell victim to the prison culture.

Billy, a country lad I knew through Go-Lab, ended up relapsing, taking acid, and trying to collect money from one of the brothers. When the brother told him, "Get lost, white boy! I ain't payin' you shit," Billy stabbed him in the stomach with his shank. When he let go of the knife, the brother pulled it out of himself and stabbed Billy to death. The consensus among the inmates was that Billy's mistake was he got too high and should have made sure the brother was dead before letting go of the weapon. No one seemed to consider that maybe the real problem was that violence was the only language these caged animals understood. Not long after Billy's demise, I witnessed another Go-Lab graduate fleeing the dining area as a fellow inmate chased him down with a butcher knife. Apparently, he died behind the chow hall when a major artery in his neck was slashed— all because he owed five bucks for a nickel bag of pot. The crazy part was that no one was even fazed by this. The law of the jungle was that if you disrespected someone, you got what you deserved.

With six months of being dry under my belt and my job at Go-Lab, I felt like I was light years beyond the other inmates. It took another con to remind me that I too had spent most of my life using violence to get my way. One day after talking trash about some yahoos who had just knocked off one of the other prisoners, I proclaimed, "The only thing wrong with me is that I drink too much every once in a while."

The other con immediately gave me a much-needed dose of reality by pointing out, "Yeah, that's why you have a life sentence—you drink too much every once in while."

I kept silent and sulked the rest of the afternoon. His comment really got under my skin. I couldn't get it out of my head and kept thinking about it for days. I wondered if maybe my problems weren't just caused by my drinking, but by my thinking as well. The past few months in Go-Lab helped me realize that I needed to change my attitude, but I had considered that a separate issue from my struggle with alcohol. Suddenly, I began to realize that everything was inter-connected. There was more to being sober than just staying dry. It meant changing your entire approach to life—and if I really wanted to achieve sobriety, I had a lot more work to do. So I pulled out the *Big Book* yet again and started reading,

One of the ways I tried to keep myself out of trouble was by play-ing softball in the prison league. On an early day in May, I was play-ing first base when a guy named Fuzzy hit a ground ball that went about five feet in front of home plate. The catcher scrambled to snatch the ball and threw it to me as Fuzzy came bearing down on the base and me. He was a little inside the line, where my glove was, and a split second after I caught the ball he came slamming into my glove. After hearing a cracking noise that sounded like a .22 caliber gunshot, an unbelievable amount of pain shot up my arm. When I looked down, I found my shoulder and three quarters of my upper left arm hanging limply in front of my chest, while my elbow, fore-arm, wrist, and hand were behind my back. My arm was literally broken in half.

Using my right hand I tried to put my arm back in place, then carefully laid down on the ground, holding my injured arm as if it was in a sling. As soon as I hit the ground a bunch of my fellow inmates came running up. "Oh man! That looks so painful," said one of the cons.

"Don't worry, we're getting help for you right now!" another one assured me.

Moments later four inmates came running up with a stretcher and gently put me on it. As they carried me to the clinic, a guard strode up alongside me.

"What did you do to yourself, boy?" he snickered.

In shock from the pain, I couldn't answer. When he saw how I cringed as each bump shot excruciating pain from my arm right up to my brain, he began knocking into the stretcher every few feet—just to increase my agony.

"Cut it out!" growled one of the inmates.

"Shut up lowlife," snapped the guard.

"Knock it off or you're going to have a problem with all of us," threatened another con.

"Yeah, lay off him!" the other inmates chimed in.

After jabbing me one more time, the guard backed off from our little parade. I tried to get a real good look at him so I could be sure to remember his face. I swore to myself that as soon as I was healed up I was going to take his life.

Forty-five minutes after arriving at the clinic, the doctor concluded that my arm was broken. "No kidding!" I muttered under my breath. I didn't need him to tell me that. I was sent off to Lake Butler Reception Center, which was about eighteen miles away. Luckily the EMT in the ambulance wasn't a sadist like the guard. When he saw the pain I was in he broke out the morphine and gave me a shot.

It took six hours for the Lake Butler doctor to determine that I had a broken arm, then he shipped me off to Alachua General, a regular hospital located thirty miles away in Gainesville. After another three hours and a shot of morphine, an orthopedic surgeon informed me that my arm was already healing crookedly. To try to pull everything back in place, he put my entire arm into a heavy cast. I was then brought back to Lake Butler and pumped up with painkillers.

A blurry week later, I went to see the surgeon again. "So, Mr. Broom, your arm is healing, but the upper arm will probably end up being crooked," he explained. "Do you think you can live with it that way?"

"Will it affect my golf swing?" I asked, half-jokingly.

Looking at me as if I was crazy, he answered, "Uh, yes."

"Then I want it straightened out!" I demanded.

"Okay, but that means I will have to rebreak your humerus and keep it in place with a metal plate . . ." the surgeon warned me.

Without a moment's hesitation, I declared, "Let's do it!

With that, the doctor scheduled me for surgery the following Monday. I was back in Alachua General on Sunday to be prepped for the following morning's surgery. I got there around 11:00 AM and spent the day enjoying my nonprison status: watching TV, making phone calls to the family, and eating the best meals I'd had since going to prison.

There were three other prisoners in the room with me, two others from the state and one from Alachua County. Around 8:30 that night I was watching the boob tube while the state guard slept in a chair in the middle of the room. A female guard from county came into the room and asked, "Excuse me, sir. Would you mind if I used your phone?"

After realizing that she wasn't kidding, I told her, "Sure!"

She picked up the phone, dialed, and turned her back to me. "Hi, honey, it's Mom . . . Yes, did you make your brother dinner? Good, now what time did he go to sleep? I know, he always does that." As she chatted away with her teenage daughter, her .38 caliber revolver hung a mere foot away from my head. I glanced over at the other guard who was fast asleep and back at the gun in the woman's holster that was within arm's reach. I couldn't believe it! It would be so easy to snag her gun, shoot sleeping piggy, and get the hell out of the hospital. I began to run the scheme through my head, imagining life on the run with a crooked arm. The thought of freedom was tempting, but I knew I would probably have to hurt more innocent people along the way and I really didn't want to do that. For five full minutes the lady cop yapped away, completely oblivious to the fact that I could have taken her out in a split second. For some reason, I didn't.

About a half hour after she got off the phone, I called her over to my bed. "Listen, ma'am. You should know that while you were talking with your daughter on my phone, you had your gun right in front of my face. I could have easily taken it from you and gotten the hell out of here. If I was another prisoner, you might well be dead right now."

As I told her this, the blood drained from her face and her hands began to tremble. She thanked me for telling her, and continued to thank me multiple times before her shift was over. Although I had missed out on what would probably be my one opportunity to escape, I felt a different sense of freedom because I had acted like a decent human being for the first time in a long while.

The next day I had the operation and everything went well according to the bone doctor. I stayed at Alachua for four days and was then shipped back to Lake Butler to recover. They kept me there for nine weeks. I guess they wanted to make sure that I would be able to protect myself before sending me back to the zoo. I was costing the state some big bucks, but I figured I was worth it.

In early August I was sent back to the Rock. I was nervous that they were going to put me through that newcomer bullshit again, but luckily I went right back to the South West Unit and Go-Lab. It was good to see my coworkers again and I immediately got back into the swing of things.

Eager to pick up where I left off, I pulled out the *Big Book* again and started doing what it called "working the steps." First, I admitted that I was powerless over alcohol and that my life had become unmanageable. Having to submit to a higher power was a challenge since I still didn't believe in God. So I decided to define my higher power as the people I went to meetings with, who people affectionately dubbed "Group Of Drunks." It seemed to work for me because, just like the book said, when I turned to my higher power for help it showed me how to stay sober.

I also took a long hard look at my life and tried to honestly identify all the defects in my personality. According to the book, I was supposed to share my story and defects with someone else. This was tough because I really didn't trust anyone. I decided to break my story up and share different parts of it with a dozen different cons. At least this way no one knew too much about me so they couldn't use anything against me. In order to make amends for what I had done, I wrote a list of all the people I had harmed over the years. That sure took a while! I then began to write letters of apology to some of them. Each day I took a hard look at myself and called myself out when I was angry, self-centered, afraid, or lying. I also honestly tried to help people who were struggling with the same demons I was.

In addition to Go-Lab and meetings, I started participating in another program called Substance Abuse: Phase 4, which was really group therapy. I was supposed to go for twelve weeks and ended up going for a year. I learned a lot about how my irrational thinking caused me problems over the years and worked on trying to think more rationally when confronting various situations. All of these efforts helped me really start to change. I admitted that I had more problems than just not being able to handle my liquor, and I was beginning to face them head-on.

I even went so far as becoming an officer in our Twelve-Step program. First I replaced someone on our steering committee, and then I was made recording secretary. Not long after that I was approached by the inside sponsor, who was actually one of the counselors from my therapy group.

"Hey, Richard, I have an idea!" she said with a big smile on her face.

"What are you thinking, Betty?" I asked, having no idea what she was going to say.

"Okay, hear me out. I don't know if you've noticed, but apparently Chairman George was showing up for meetings completely in the tank."

I started to laugh. "Yeah, I think he's been drunk for just about every meeting I've been to."

"Yes, well, it's not really going over well with our outside sponsors, and I think his time is up. There's an election coming up and I think you should run for cochair."

"Are you joking?" I replied, stunned. "Who the hell am I to run the meetings? Plus, there hasn't been a white chairman in over nineteen years!"

"First of all, you are more than qualified," she argued. "You've been extremely active at all our meetings and are running almost a hundred different Go-Lab lectures. You know how to do this. And as far as the racial issue is concerned, you should run with Toby Brown. I think he can take the black vote!"

Toby was an ex–Black Panther, so I guess he did have some pull with the black members. "But George's ticket," I tried to argue.

"George's ticket is just divisive," Betty interrupted. "His running mate Louis is part of Yahweh, that black supremacist group out of Miami. There's not a chance in hell that any of the white guys will vote for him. Listen to me, George is played out. Everyone is looking for some new blood around here, and you and Toby can bring that to the table. If you win, Toby could serve for the first year so you could take that time to learn from him; then you'd feel more comfortable when your term came up. What do you say, are you in?"

Swept up in Betty's enthusiasm, I cheered, "I'm in!"

Three weeks later I found myself participating in a debate in front of three hundred members. George was on stage giving the same speech he made for the past three elections and everyone in the audience seemed bored. When Toby got up to speak, he seemed to capture everyone's attention. He was then followed by Louis, who gave a fiery speech that was hard to ignore. He even went as far as to say that he would be willing to die for our program—which I found interesting, if not stupid.

It was my turn to take the stage, and as I walked up I thought about how I felt the first time I went up there to read "How it Works." I was so much more confident now and attributed it to the fact that I knew I just had to keep it honest—and that's just what I did. In response to Louis's comment, I told the crowd, "I don't know about anyone else, but I came to this Twelve-Step program so I could live." I was greeted with a roar of approval, and we ended up winning the election—capturing at least half the black vote.

I would only be the cochair for about six months because I was finally granted a transfer out of Raiford. I tried to switch to Dade Correctional because they had a Go-Lab program there, but my classification officer told me that option was out. I could go to Avon Park instead. Desperate to go to a less violent place, I took his offer, and by the end of April 1986, I said good-bye to the Rock forever. I would finally be able to walk ten feet without looking over my shoulder to see what danger lurked behind me. It was time to start looking forward.

Chapter Twenty-Four

AFTER A FOUR-HOUR RIDE, OUR BUS PULLED UP TO an air force checkpoint and passed through a bombing range before arriving at my new home, Avon Park Correctional Institution. This time, rather than being threatened by jeering convicts, we were greeted by friendly guards who promptly removed our leg and waist chains. After being ushered into a large room, we were addressed by the prison's assistant superintendent.

"Welcome to Avon Park, boys," he said with a thick southern accent. "If y'all comin' from Raiford, you gonna find this place real laid back. We don't put up with any violence 'round here. So if any of you think y'all gonna start trouble, think again. You'll be shipped right back to the zoo to be with the other animals at Raiford or Marion Correctional.

"Believe me, I know everything that goes on around here. Jimmy Brown, Bobby Jackson, Derek Roy, and Garrett Thompson are workin' for me and will tell me if anything goes down. And if you even think about laying a hand on any of them, you will not only be

removed from Avon Park, but y'all be tried for assault and battery—
or whatever charge we deem convictable."

I couldn't believe that he was actually telling us who his snitches
were. While it bothered me that they had so much pull, I did like the
idea that there wouldn't be any violence.

"And another thing," he added. "Don't be messing with any of the
bugs 'round here. Ya'll just leave them alone." Of course, he didn't
mean insects; he was talking about the inmates who were on psychotropic meds.

After the pep talk, I found out that I was assigned to room 212 in
C-building where I would be sharing a cell with a charming fellow
named Hacksaw, a speed freak who ran into trouble while babysitting a pot farm outside of Gainesville. In addition to his insatiable
appetite for pot and meth, his time spent fighting in Vietnam fueled
his regular bouts of paranoia. In the heat of an argument, the pot
grower Hacksaw was working for pulled a gun on him, so he took
the farmer out with his double-barreled shotgun. While there was
no question that he was simply defending himself, Hacksaw was still
stuck with a dead body in the middle of a giant pot farm. He wasn't
about to call the cops—especially while high on meth. He did what
anyone would do: he pulled out his hacksaw and cut the body into
pieces and then buried them in shallow holes around the farm.
Unfortunately for Hacksaw, when the cops came looking for the
farmer, they stumbled across a finger sticking up out of the dirt.
Hacksaw ended up with a life sentence and a mandatory minimum
of twenty-five years. Still haunted by Vietnam, burnt out from the
meth, and furious with the justice system, he spent his time in Avon
Park running at least five miles a day. Hacksaw was getting ready to
make a run for it, but for now, he was my new roomie.

I quickly established a healthy routine at Avon Park. When I wasn't
working at the dental clinic, I went to Twelve-Step meetings and
started exercising regularly. Afternoons consisted of lifting weights,

shooting hoops, and running, while my evenings were spent playing either softball or basketball. My nights were spent reading until 2:00 AM. I did my best to keep busy, play by the rules, and continue to grow.

Some of the guards were really cool to us, like the one who let me read in the hallway every night after lights out. But there was one guard who, for some unknown reason, had it out for the inmates who went to the Twelve-Step meetings. Every time we entered the visiting park for our weekly meeting he would call us scum of the earth, pieces of shit, or whatever other derogatory name he could think of at the time. Ironically, after a year of his weekly tirades, his daughter was killed in a drunk driving accident on her graduation night. She was drinking and driving, lost control of her car, and died.

His story, as well as many others—including my own—got me thinking more about karma. It became clearer and clearer to me that what goes around comes around. Recognizing this helped me realize that I didn't have to get even with other people; I could always count on cosmic justice to eventually even the score.

My personal spiritual journey got a major kick in the ass one afternoon at Avon Park. I was sitting in my cell around 2:30, reading a novel, when my cell suddenly filled up with smoke. I started sniffing around, trying to figure out where it was coming from, but I couldn't smell the smoke nor could I see any fire. After a few moments, I realized that the smoke wasn't really there—it was just in my head.

Oh no! I thought to myself, *I'm going blind! Now I won't even be able to read!*

A minute later, I heard a voice saying, "Everything will be alright, Dickie." I stood still. It was the voice of my Nanny, but it was how her voice sounded twenty-five years ago. Again I heard her, "Everything will be alright, Dickie."

I never should have taken that acid way back when, I said to myself. I was convinced that I was having a flashback. I kept hearing her, over and over, telling me that everything was going to be alright. Suddenly the voice faded away and the smoke cleared from eyes.

Seeing clearly again, I started to shiver. I looked around to see if anyone had seen my freak out. No one was watching. Wondering what the hell that was all about, I told myself again that it must have been inspired by some LSD I had taken years ago. I tried to start reading again, but had a hard time concentrating. I just couldn't shake an uneasy feeling about what had just happened.

The following afternoon, around the same time, I was back in my cell when a guard summoned me up to the administration building. It was never a good sign to be called up front, and I tried to figure out what I had done wrong or who might be trying to set me up. I kept drawing a blank because I couldn't think of any rule I had broken.

When I walked into the building, a guard barked at me, "Call your parents on the phone."

I pointed to the phone on a nearby desk and asked, "That one?"

"Yeah, that one, stupid!" snarled the guard. "Do you see any other fucking phones in here?"

I bit my tongue, walked over to the desk, and picked up the receiver. Before dialing, I asked the guard, "Do I need to dial anything to get out of here?"

"Just dial the phone!" the guard exploded.

I did what I was told and my mom answered the phone. "Hi, Mom. It's Richard."

Without missing a beat, she bluntly said, "Nanny died yesterday afternoon around 2:30."

A chill ran down my spine. Aside from the feelings of sadness over her being gone and guilt for not being there for her over the years, I was completely blown away by what had happened the day before. The guard rushed me off the phone before I could get any more details on exactly what had happened, and I was hustled back to my cell.

Looking out through the barred windows of my cell, I pondered what had occurred the day before. Nanny must have been saying good-bye to me and somehow she saw the future and knew it was going to be okay. Of course, still the self-centered son of a bitch that I was, I was frustrated because she didn't tell me how soon things would turn around for me, or how long would it be before I got out of prison.

The incident did make me think that I better hedge my bets and start praying. Obviously there was something happening in the afterlife, and I realized I better get my shit together quick to make up for all the lost time I'd spent raising hell. I wasn't going to go crazy and start hanging around the chapel, but I was definitely going to start praying. I wasn't really sure who I was talking to, but I was pretty sure someone was listening. The only problem was that I only knew two prayers: the Lord's Prayer and the one that starts with, "Now I lay me down to sleep, I pray the Lord my soul to keep . . . "

Once I started praying my two prayers every night, a major shift happened in my life. Before that date every time someone offered me booze, I would have to fight it. In my Twelve-Step meetings they would call that "white knuckle sobriety." Yet, after I started praying, I no longer felt a rush when someone offered me a drink. I didn't have to fight off my cravings; they were gone. Alcohol didn't mean anything to me any more. I had tried to do this on my own, without any luck. Somehow this higher power that everyone kept talking about at meetings seemed to work.

I came to believe that the Twelve-Step program was what would keep me out of prison if I ever got out. I would even say that it played a big role in keeping me from becoming "institutionalized." Shrinks, social workers, and other people in the justice system throw that term around when talking about people who become so accustomed to the prison culture that they don't know how to survive on the outside. Supposedly, it takes about five years for this to happen, but my involvement with the Twelve-Step group kept me connected to the world beyond my prison cell.

When I became chairman of the group, I was responsible for setting up the annual banquet held in the prison cafeteria. This project made me remember that I could do more than time. As chairman and someone with restaurant experience, I decided that this banquet was going to be different from the usual ones held every year. At every one I went to during my years on the inside, we'd get prison food, which was usually disgusting chicken—or what the cons called "barnyard pimp." I decided that this year we would have something special, using ingredients brought in from outside the prison. I didn't have a big budget, so I decided on serving Monte Carlo sandwiches. In order to set everything up, I had to hop on the phone and call a bunch of different companies and order everything we needed to make over one hundred sandwiches. I felt like I was ordering for one of the places I used to work for, and it made me feel like a real person again—at least while I was on the phone.

I also brought in a special speaker, an old friend of mine from New York, Donny. Back in the day Donny was a wild man, working as a bartender at a college gin mill and chasing every skirt he could. Once he got sober, he pulled himself together and got his master's degree in social work. Now he was working as a counselor at an alcohol and drug rehab in the West Palm Beach area. While I was in jail, he built a worthwhile life for himself and I was proud of him. When I asked him to come speak to our group, he didn't hesitate for a moment. He drove two and half hours, ate his sandwich, potato salad, and dill pickle, and spoke to us cons for forty-five minutes. He reminded us that people in Twelve-Step programs came from all walks of life. They could be from Park Place or the park bench. Everyone in the program had one thing in common, though: they couldn't control their drinking or using. The banquet went smoothly and I felt a genuine sense of pride and accomplishment for pulling it off. I think it gave the other inmates a sense of dignity and hope too.

All good things must come to an end. One morning I was woken up early, along with four hundred other inmates, and told to pack my shit because I was being transferred. Apparently some whiny bitch kept filing lawsuits against the staff at Avon Park because he wanted better medical care. In order to get rid of the headache, the prison decided to move him and all the other prisoners who were identified as Medical 3s and 4s—which referred to the inmates who weren't supposed to do any physical labor. I fell under the Medical 3 classification because of my softball injury, so I was forced to move on out as well.

Within an hour, twenty-five other inmates and I were stuffed into a steamy, stinking van. All the seats had been taken out to squeeze in more people, so we stood shackled and bent over for the entire two-hour drive. We were dumped off in front of Sumter Correctional Institute, a youth prison where most of the inmates were under twenty-five years old and on meds. All I could think was: *Damn, karma's a bitch.*

Chapter Twenty-Five

SINCE THE CELLS IN SUMTER WERE RESERVED FOR solitary confinement, I ended up in a dormitory-style building with endless rows of bunk beds where you never got any privacy. There was no air-conditioning, so the windows were open all the time. When the wind blew in we could smell the wonderful aroma of chicken shit from the farm down the road. Along with the smell came hundreds of flies, which would buzz from bed to bed. I was back in hell.

To escape the dorm and get into some air-conditioning, I immediately got a job working in the medical clinic. While there I met a psychologist who read my file and knew that I was in a Twelve-Step program. He asked me to help him restart the program in Sumter. By this time I hadn't had a drink in over four and a half years, but I recognized that this place was such a nightmare that I might slip up if I didn't keep working the steps. I knew I needed the program to keep sane, so I agreed to help him out. Within a few weeks we had over a dozen people coming to the group.

Still determined to get the hell out of Sumter, I contacted Stephen Jordan, my parole lawyer, to see what he could do. I'd already paid him five grand from money Nanny left me to work on the parole board. That meant he was supposed to make sure that I would get out within the standard guidelines, which was a maximum of eight years and four months for a first offense life sentence.

After being transferred to Sumter, I paid Stephen even more to try to get me into an easier facility. While he agreed with me that it was unfair that I got screwed because of my medical condition, he tried to explain that it could take some time to straighten everything out. Of course, patience was never one of my strong points, but I did my best to sit tight and stay out of trouble. Stephen kept telling me that one of the stipulations for me to get out within the standard guidelines was that I had to have a clean prison record. My record was spotless up until this point, but Sumter was the kind of place where you could find trouble without even looking for it.

Take the guy in the bunk right next to me. He was a Mexican who didn't speak any Spanish, but he would have been picked out of central casting to play Poncho Villa. After getting a three-year sentence for marijuana possession, he was back in business smuggling cocaine into the prison. Every morning around 5:30 AM he would head out to the yard on garbage duty. In addition to picking up litter, he was collecting aluminum arrows filled with cocaine that were shot into the yard overnight. Poncho would deliver the arrows to the inside distributor who would then pay Poncho, bag the blow, and sell it around the prison. Even though I was straight at the time, I was impressed with the operation—it was sheer genius.

I met another coke dealer in the medical clinic one afternoon. A short little wheeler-dealer, he told me his tale of woe about getting busted with three kilos in West Palm Beach. As a matter of prison etiquette, I shared my saga with him, and as we parted ways I thought that was the end of the story. It wasn't.

The next day I was sitting in the chow hall when someone I knew from Raiford came running up to me. "Holy shit, Broom! I just heard some con saying that you were the guy who killed his partner. You better watch your ass, man. He was talking a lot of smack about paybacks and he's definitely juicing himself up to do something."

I knew that when in the jungle, it's best to make the first move. I had already done six years and wasn't about to get stabbed in the back by Daniel's partner in crime. So the next time I caught the prick from West Palm Beach in the chow hall, I cornered him. Looking him right in the eyes, I growled, "Are you thinkin' about doing something?"

"No," he answered, looking away from me.

"Look me straight in the eyes and tell me if you're thinking about doing something" I demanded.

When he finally met my gaze, I saw nothing but fear in his eyes and I knew he wished he'd never said a word about knowing I was his partner's killer. "No," he claimed. "I don't have anything on my mind."

While I thought he probably meant it and I wouldn't have to worry about him sticking a shank in my back, I decided to still keep an eye on him. I didn't have to watch him for long. That very night he put himself in protective custody and that was the last time I saw him. I was lucky that he was gone because either I would have ended up dead or in deep shit for defending myself.

Trouble finally caught up with me when I got swept up in a fight after some black guys robbed a bunch of white inmates' lockers. I tried to stay cool at first, even though my locker was broken into as well. I simply told the fuckers that I was not happy about it and would find out which small-time crooks were stealing. But later on that day, a young white kid with the build of a linebacker found out who the thief was and went after him in the TV room. Seconds after they started fighting they were surrounded by thirty other cons, mostly black. It was a fairly even fight. The black kid, who was six-feet, three-inches and about 205 pounds, was winning the fight—probably because of his speed; but the white boy was tenacious.

As the fight went on another one of the brothers tried to sneak-attack the white boy from behind. When he snuck up, I angled toward the little cheap-shot artist and he backed off once he saw me. We played this game a couple more times, and the last time I grabbed him and held him back so he couldn't move. Moments later the guards charged in and broke up the fight.

A half hour later I was in my bunk when Cheap Shot came up behind me with a broomstick in his hand. "Cracker," he threatened, "if you ever try and stop me again I'll bust your mother-fuckin' head open!"

Now I knew the guy was trying to save face, but I had had enough of his bullshit. When I pushed the bunks apart and started toward him, he was surprised and started backing up. I kept coming at him and he found himself a good thirty feet from where we started. He had no where else to go. As I went to disarm the little punk, his buddy came out of nowhere with a mop handle and whacked me across the temple and ear on the right side of my head. I went down quick and hard and attempted to cover my head—even though I was almost knocked out. I tried to move but my body wasn't listening to my brain. I just lay there as the two street punks pounded me with their broom and mop handles. It lasted for a minute or two before a thirty-two-year-old Mr. T look-alike stopped them.

The guards finally showed up a few minutes later and dragged us all in front of the captain, who decided to toss us all into solitary until he could figure out what had happened.

"Great!" I scowled as the guards escorted me out of his office. "Punish the victim!"

My commentary was not considered helpful and I ended up spending a week in solitary. When I finally got in touch with

Stephen he promised to get me out of Sumter and transferred to Lake Correctional, a peaceful place like Avon Park. A week later I was put on a bus for transfer, but I never made it to Lake Correctional Institute. They brought me to Marion Correctional instead. When I got off the bus I was pissed. I had paid Stephen over ten grand and I ended up at one of the most violent prisons in the Florida system. Again I was living in a sweltering dorm and the temperature was topping out at close to 95 degrees every day for the first three weeks I was there.

The saving grace of Marion was that there were four Twelve-Step meetings held each week. I immediately started going to them. I also found refuge in the beautiful new library. It was filled with thousands of novels, including a bunch of them from writers I'd been trying to find. I began reading a novel a day, escaping the harsh reality of Marion—through the imaginations of talented authors rather than the bottle.

I did everything I could to establish a healthy routine. I even asked for work in the kitchen because I wanted to have the afternoons free to exercise or go to the library. My classification officer, who was already impressed with my prison record, gladly granted my request.

Sitting in a Twelve-Step meeting one evening, I was struck with an "Aha!" moment. While listening to someone speak, I suddenly realized that I had more freedom sober in prison than I did drunk on the street. Although I couldn't go anywhere, I could think anything, believe anything, or feel anything I wanted to. Caught up in the excitement of this realization, I raised my hand and asked to come up to the podium to share my thoughts. When I got up there, I declared, "Of course I'd rather be sober on the street, but if there was only one choice, I'd rather be sober in prison than drunk on the street."

"What a kiss-ass!" complained one of the other inmates.

"Your opinion is your opinion, but I bet that you probably haven't taken an honest look at your own lives," I countered as many of the other cons chimed in with boos and catcalls. "I'm just saying that maybe you ought to think about how you landed in here and whether or not booze was involved."

Most of the guys there were shredding me, but I knew where they were coming from. Appearing vulnerable could be a death sentence in prison. Acting tough was a survival skill. Still, there were a few guys at the meeting who seemed to nod their heads in agreement with what I was saying, including two volunteers from the local Twelve-Step group and another inmate who seemed to go to every meeting I did. After the meeting, the three of them came up to me.

"That took a lot of courage to say what you said," said the inmate.

"Yeah," agreed one of the volunteers. "It was really brave to share like that."

"It wasn't courage," I responded quietly. "It was just the truth." I didn't tell them that it was actually sort of a spiritual awakening for me. I knew that in order for me to get out prison and stay out of prison, I had to act differently and the time to start was now.

My commitment to change was tested soon after that night when I spotted Mr. Cheap Shot who had attacked me with the broomstick back in Sumter. My first impulse was to grab a large rock and smash his skull with it. Luckily, I decided to think before I acted. By the time I thought it over, Cheap Shot was in the chow hall and it was too late to do anything anyway.

Although I tried to let it go, the next morning I found myself hiding behind a row of pine trees outside the dining hall, waiting to bash his head in and send him off to the medical clinic. The fucker was responsible for me being stuck in this hellhole. Cheap Shot deserved to feel the same pain I did when he and his cowardly friend jumped me. I guess my higher power, whatever the hell that is, was looking over me that day, because Cheap Shot never came to breakfast. I never got a chance to get myself into trouble.

When I finally came to my senses, I decided to try handling the situation like a mature adult. I went to my classification officer and told him everything about what had happened in Sumter. I confessed that I had considered a sneak attack to get my revenge but decided to confide in him instead. I wasn't sure how it was going to play out, but I felt that being honest was the best approach.

Within three hours, I was watching three classification officers going off on Mr. Cheap Shot. My classification officer began by pointing at me and asking, "Do you know who he is?"

"Yes," the brother snipped.

"Do you know why he is here?" probed another officer.

"No," Cheap Shot muttered.

The two officers I didn't know got up and came to his side of the table. One of them towered over him while the other leaned over and got in his face. "Do you have any ill feelings toward him?"

"No," he whispered.

"Now listen closely, boy. If anything happens to Mr. Broom— anything at all—you will be held responsible and will be prosecuted for it," threatened one of the officers. "Even if he falls and hurts himself jogging, it's on your head. Got it?"

"Yessir," he shuddered.

I began to feel bad for the kid. He was getting a rash of shit and he hadn't even done anything yet, but I knew that he was better off dealing with them than with me. I knew I did the right thing, and it felt good to be on the right side of the law for once.

After the meeting, my classification officer called me into his office. "Sit down, Richard. I wanted to let you know that this afternoon I had a conversation with your lawyer and you will be going to Lake Correctional in the next few days. I hate losing you, as you have been a model inmate. But you need to get out of here and go to a less violent camp. The truth is you are too good for Marion."

I almost fell out of my seat. I couldn't remember the last time I was given a compliment and, I have to say, I liked it. Maybe I didn't have to live by the laws of jungle.

"Also, I look forward to putting in a good word for you during your next parole hearing," he smiled.

The thought of having a life beyond the prison walls was something I tried not to think about over the years, but it started to seem as if it was in reach. My parole hearing wasn't for another twenty months, but now it didn't feel that far away. After changing my way of thinking and acting, adjusting my outlook and attitudes, I began to believe that I might just be able to live in the real world and be happy. I just hoped that someday I would be given the chance.

Lake Correctional was like a country club compared to other prisons I'd been in. There weren't any gun towers. There was a lake to go fishing instead. It was a place I could easily tolerate. Hell, they even had two Twelve-Step meetings a week, and within two months I was voted in as cochairman of our group. I also ran into Bill from Go-Lab at Raiford, and he hooked me up with a job as secretary for the electrical department.

As soon as I started my job, I set up a manageable routine that included time spent reading, going to meetings, praying, and working out. Staying busy seemed to be an effective way to keep myself out of trouble, and after being transferred around so many times I was getting good at setting up a routine. Plus, it helped to pass the time.

Before I knew it, Stephen paid me a visit and gave me the best news I'd heard in years. "The Department of Corrections is placing a program called PROP (Pre-Release Orientation Program) in several work release centers," he said, "and they're looking for Go-Lab instructors to work in the program." Stephen smiled. "Any interest in working as an instructor at the Opa-Locka Community Release Center in Dade County, right next to Miami?"

"Hell yes!" I boomed.

"Now, this place is a work release center, but you will still only be on the inside. You wouldn't be on release—"

"I don't care!" I cut him off. "At least I won't be living in this damn prison anymore!"

"Okay, I should be able to make this happen pretty quickly. Oh, and you'll also be meeting with a representative from the parole commission in the next couple of weeks. Most likely they will lower your parole date to be within five years. Plus your custody would be lowered to minimum custody."

I was one step closer to freedom.

Chapter Twenty-Six

I T WAS LATE IN THE AFTERNOON ON A WARM MAY IN 1989 when I arrived at the work release center in Opa-Locka. The place was nothing like any of the other prisons I'd been in. It was a minimum custody facility, so there were no fences, and from the outside it looked like a motel. The rooms inside were freshly painted with new tiles on the floor, and the bathrooms had porcelain fixtures rather than cold steel. My room was fairly large and I had it all to myself.

Lying in bed on my first night there, I felt great. I was finally on my way out of this nightmare. Within a couple of years I'd be on parole. There was a light at the end of the tunnel. Genuinely relaxed for the first time in years, I peacefully drifted off to sleep.

Three hours later I was brought back to reality when a guard with a German shepherd came bursting into the room. "Stay in bed!" yelled the guard.

I felt my whole body tense up as soon as I heard the guard's voice. He sounded just like someone from Raiford. "What the hell is going on?" I asked as politely as I could.

"The Dade County evidence building next door was broken into," he responded irritably as his mutt nosed through all my stuff. "Brutus here is a narcotics officer and we're here to nail the dumb fuck who did it."

Unsure of who was a greater threat, the dog or the guard, I did my best to stay still. I hadn't done anything, but I didn't want to make a false move and have either of them come after me. Then, as quickly as they appeared, they were gone. The next morning, over some breakfast slop, I got confirmation that the guard used to work at the Rock. I'd thought all that nonsense was behind me now that I was in this shiny new place, but apparently not.

After breakfast I cruised over to the PROP office to find out more about my schedule. I was eager to get started running groups, even though I was apprehensive about the other leaders checking me out. I already knew 80 percent of the program from Go-Lab and was confident that I could easily learn the rest. Of course, the first thing I asked was when the Twelve-Step meetings were held. I was encouraged when I found out that not only did they have meetings every Tuesday night at the center, inmates could also go to outside meetings in Key Biscayne on Friday and Sunday nights.

The first outside meeting I went to was on a Sunday night. There I met Jimmy O'C., a seemingly hardworking, stable guy from Philadelphia with almost three years of clean time. I found out that night that he had a penchant for straightening out for a couple years and getting his life together, then sabotaging everything by relapsing. As he spoke, I thought about our drunken chairperson back at Raiford who preached about "not leaving your Twelve-Step program at the gate." Although he was a complete hypocrite, his message still mattered. I hadn't even considered relapsing, and the thought of it scared the hell out of me. I never wanted to be out of control again. I vowed to myself that I would do whatever it took to prevent that from happening.

The following Friday I went to another meeting in Key Biscayne. As we drove past the posh homes, I chuckled to myself. I knew that, aside from going to a meeting, the only reason many of the inmates in our van would ever come to this neighborhood would be to rob someone's house. Most of the other people at the meeting seemed to be pretty well-off, and we didn't have much in common with them except that they were addicts too. Despite our differences, the meeting inspired me. There were some people there with over twenty years of sobriety who had plenty of wisdom to share. The structure of the meetings was cool, too. It was a speaker/discussion group where someone would tell his story about what he was like when he was drinking, what happened as a result of his behavior, and what he was like now.

After opening up and sharing during my second Friday night meeting, a guy named Bill came up to me and started chatting. Originally from Wyoming, Bill had done some pretty nasty things while he was drinking, but now that he was sober he had a desire to give back. Within minutes of meeting, he asked me, "Do you want a sponsor?"

I hesitated for about three seconds, and then jumped at the chance. It was clear that Bill had achieved a state of serenity and peace that I desperately needed. To be honest, I also wanted what he had: freedom, a slick car, and home in Key Biscayne. So I took his number and agreed to call him.

At the following meeting, Bill walked up to me, obviously disappointed. "Why did you only call me once?"

"Sorry about that," I apologized. Embarrassed, I explained. "I'm on a limited budget and don't always have a quarter for the pay phone we have to use."

Bill seemed relieved. "Oh, we can find a way to work around that. Let me ask you first, have you worked the Twelve Steps yet?"

"Yeah, twice," I said proudly. "Once out of the *Big Book* and then once with a therapist using work sheets for each step."

"But you really need to do it with a sponsor. That way, when you eventually sponsor someone else, you'll have a structured way of doing it," he countered.

"No one would ever ask me to be their sponsor," I laughed.

"You have a lot more to offer than you think, Richard," Bill pressed. Whether or not he really meant it, I fell for what he was saying. Of course, boosting my ego was usually a surefire way to get me on board. So although I thought it would be a waste of time, I agreed to do it anyway.

What I didn't know was that working the steps with a sponsor forces you to be honest with yourself—and that's exactly what Bill did for me. He made me see things I couldn't see for myself. Now, at this stage in my life, I acknowledged that out of the seven deadly sins, I was definitely guilty of false pride and anger. It was pretty obvious how they both had caused big problems for me. As for the other sins—greed, gluttony, envy, lust, and sloth—I really didn't think I was that bad. Sure, I stole money from the restaurants I worked for, but I didn't steal that much. Okay, I kept bitching about how my brother had the fancy house on the water in Connecticut. So what? Bill cut through my bullshit and made me face the fact that I was being greedy and envious. As I reviewed my life with him, he made me quit making excuses and instead acknowledge the defects in my character. And yet, no matter what I told him, he still stood by me unconditionally. He treated me like a son.

In addition to Bill, I also received a great deal of support from Tony and Steve—two other members of the Biscayne group who also brought the meetings to the work release center. Both of them were pretty well off. Tony designed the interior of yachts, and Steve was a rich boy from Los Angeles. But they were willing to reach out to cons like us.

One of the most important things they taught me was how to deal with anger and resentment. At a Monday night meeting, I voiced my feelings about Sergeant March, one of the officers at Opa-Locka. He was a fat, nasty ballbuster who spent his days giving everyone a hard time. He only screwed with me once, but he would jerk around the brothers all the time. He was obviously a total bigot, and he would push them until they snapped—then they would get shipped back to a regular prison.

When I brought up my resentment toward Sergeant March, Bill and Tony surprised me by their response. Rather than agreeing with me or reminding me of the typical anger management techniques, they suggested that I should pray for the bastard. They told me a story about a woman who had all sorts of resentments toward her mother. After praying to her higher power to help rid her of the ill feelings, she came across a magazine with a cover story on dealing with resentment. Taking this as a sign, she followed the article's suggestion to pray for the person she was angry with for fourteen days. So she prayed for her mother to receive everything she wanted for herself, like happiness, health, and prosperity. After two weeks, the woman's resentment was gone.

I took their advice, but I guess I didn't really get the message about how the praying was supposed to work. I prayed for March every night, except my prayer was that he would go to heaven . . . as soon as possible! After fourteen days of saying this prayer, nothing happened to him, although I did seem to stop paying so much attention to his antics. Then, a week later, I noticed that he hadn't been at work for a couple days. When I asked the officer in charge of PROP what was going on, she informed me that he'd suffered a major heart attack. Although he lived, he was forced to retire.

At first, I was elated by the news. What goes around comes around, right? Now the son of a bitch had to give up his favorite hobby of fucking with the inmates. While I expressed my glee in our

Twelve-Step meeting, I didn't show the full extent of the warm fuzzy feeling I was experiencing at his expense. Then something really strange happened. I began to feel something I hadn't really felt before. It took me a while to identify what it was, but eventually I realized it was guilt. Somehow I felt responsible for what had happened, even though I knew I really didn't have anything to do with fat boy's bad luck. I felt guilty because I was so elated about someone else's hardship. I was confused at first because I was never one to feel guilt. But once I realized what was going on, I actually felt good about it. *Hell, I must be getting emotionally healthy,* I thought. *I actually have a conscience now!*

Opportunities to grow continued to present themselves. A couple of weeks later, the Biscayne group asked for one of the inmates from our group to get up and share his story. A Columbian named Rafael initially volunteered to do it, but during the week leading up to the meeting, he asked me to take his place. "You're a professional speaker, man," he tried to schmooze me. "You get up and yap all the time when you're running your classes. You should be the one up there. You would represent the group better than I ever could, and we've gotta look good in front of those alkies."

"I'd be glad to do it," I said, patting him on the back. I could tell that the real reason he was asking was that he was too chicken to go up and share, but I didn't call him out on it. The truth was that I was excited to get a chance to go up in front of the group.

When Friday rolled around, I was nervous, but ready to tell my tale. Right before the meeting was about to start, we told the chairperson about the change. He didn't seem upset at all. He just said, "Richard will do. The group just wants someone from the Opa-Locka group to share and take some responsibility for the meeting. You guys are a part of the group."

Moments later the chairperson called me up to speak. Taking a deep breath, I began, "My name is Richard and I'm an alcoholic. I grew up in Albany, New York . . . " For the next forty-five minutes I shared my war stories, describing how alcohol had ruined my life and explaining how I was trying to get my life back. I spent a lot of time talking about my drinking career and what I was like as a drunk, culminating with the blackout that led to the midnight crime on July 4. I guess I really had something to say because I didn't even realize that I went fifteen minutes over my allotted time—but it didn't seem to matter. When I finished, I was greeted by a hearty round of applause, and then a number of members from the group came up to talk to me after the meeting.

"Thanks so much for sharing," said a middle-aged man in a suit.

"Thanks for being here," I answered—-and meant it from the bottom of my heart.

"I really enjoyed your story," piped in an older woman.

"Well, I didn't," I joked, and everyone burst into laughter.

For the next twenty minutes I listened to other people in the group tell me how lucky they were, and that they could have been me. From drunken brawls to being wasted behind the wheel, I heard story after story about close calls with the law. I even got a couple hugs from some of the ladies in the group. It felt great being the center of attention and I was full of myself for a short while afterwards. Not only did I find something I was good at, I was also being of service to the Twelve-Step program.

On the way back to the center, some of the other cons thanked me for making them look good—or at least human. I spent much of the drive thinking about my speech, going over what I forgot to say and what I could have said differently. I was on cloud nine and felt like I had finally arrived.

In July, another opportunity arose that would have a profound influence on my life. John, an inmate who was the chairperson of our inside group, was invited to go to the Twelve-Step group's state convention to be held at a beautiful resort nearby. When he didn't want to go, he asked me to take his place, and a week later I was off to the convention.

There were seven inmates from across the state who were invited to attend the convention. Although it was held in Hallandale, which was only fifteen miles from Opa-Locka, we were brought all the way up to West Palm Beach and transported back and forth sixty miles each way, every day. I didn't really care. All I could think about was the fact that we would have five days and evenings away from the Sergeant Marches of the world and the rest of the prison mentality. It was almost like being free—almost. At that time in my life, it was as good as it got.

We were required to attend at least one meeting per day, and then we could whatever we wanted at the resort for the rest of the time. While most of the other cons did just that, I went to three two-hour meetings, plus a couple of discussion groups every day. I didn't play in the pool or bask on the beach. I went to meetings instead.

Over 4,000 recovering people attended the event, and amazingly, they all seemed happy. I couldn't get over the fact that they could have so much fun in recovery. Everyone seemed to have a good time, especially the speakers. Some of them were so hilarious they could have been stand-up comedians.

I also met up with a number of people I knew, including Donny, my old pal from Albany, who was working as a therapist in an alcohol and drug rehab in West Palm Beach. I ran into Tom, from Go-Lab in Raiford, who was now out on parole, as well. Unfortunately, I didn't get a chance to talk to him because it was ten o'clock and I had to get to the appointed pickup spot to head back to West Palm Beach. On the ride back, I tried to think about how glad I was for Tom to be free, but I couldn't help but feel somewhat envious too. While I was getting closer and closer to freedom, it still seemed so far away. I wasn't out yet and one wrong move could set me back indefinitely.

Closing ceremonies were the next day, and I kept on the lookout for Tom but never spotted him. I tried to make the most out of every last moment there, listening intently to the final speaker. While I felt an overwhelming sense of sadness as we said the closing prayer, I was also so grateful for the five days there. Throughout the convention many of the speakers talked about the importance of gratitude, and it hit me that I needed to begin to acknowledge the positive things happening in my life. I was sober, I had made it to a work release facility, I was able to attend four meetings a week, and I had built up a support system to keep me on a positive course. Life was getting better all the time.

The connections I made through my Twelve-Step groups made an enormous difference when I found out that the state was transferring the entire PROP program over to Miami North, another work release center near the airport. After five months of getting comfortable at Opa-Locka, it was time to adjust to a whole new set of rules. Luckily, by this time I had a network of people from various Twelve-Step programs to get me through it. Bill was always there for me, as was Jimmy O'C. and many other people I knew. I also met a whole new group of volunteers, including a bunch of bikers who would drive us to outside meetings.

As usual, there was a guard who had it out for me. At Miami North it was Officer Kumin. For some unknown reason, he thought I was a con artist and was always trying to catch me doing something wrong. I'd be in the PROP office preparing a lesson plan and he would charge in ready to bust me for something. He never caught me because I was never doing anything I wasn't supposed to. I think that frustrated the hell out of him. Mrs. V., the woman in charge of the PROP program, tried to tell him that I was for real and was genuinely trying to improve myself, but he wasn't buying it. I spent most of my time trying to avoid him. Although I had come a long way, I was still human. I didn't want to screw myself by having an unnecessary run-in with a loser like him.

It ended up being a smart move to stay out of trouble, because I had a parole hearing less than five months after moving to Miami North. Miraculously, everything seemed to go my way. My parole date was lowered to April 4, 1991, and I was made eligible to go on work release. That meant that I could finally work on the outside. I immediately requested a move to Beckham Hall in Miami. The living conditions weren't that great there, but according to the convict grapevine, the staff was loose and the place was wide open. Rumor had it that you could do whatever you wanted. Although I had come so far, I had yet to prove to myself that I could overcome temptation and stay clean and sober when living on the outside. This was going to be the true test.

Chapter Twenty-Seven

ALTHOUGH BECKHAM HALL WAS A DUMP IN A run-down section of Miami, the inmates liked to go there because they could get away with a lot more than they could at Opa-Locka or Miami North. It was relatively easy to screw around during the day when you were supposed to be working. Some of the cons would get a job at a Mom and Pop store in their old neighborhood, and then spend their days on the corner selling crack instead. Mom and Pop would cover for them as long as they got a slice of the pie. The night guards were also on the take—nothing big, but for twenty bucks they would ignore the fact that you were out all night. It was a damn free-for-all. The administrators didn't seem to give a shit. The assistant chief and her boss were rumored to have alcohol and cocaine habits, and the assistant chief was doing one of the inmates.

Ironically, my choice to avoid getting involved in the hoopla actually made me stand out from the rest of the inmates. Shortly after I arrived, the assistant chief brought me into her office. "I see you requested to come to Beckham Hall. Why would you want to come here?" she asked as she looked over my file.

I decided to tell the truth. "I heard this place was wide open and figured if I could stay sober here, I could stay sober when I got out. I thought it would be a good test for me."

She looked at me as if I was crazy. "Well, then . . . I, uh, appreciate your honesty." Knowing that she often showed up weak in the knees after her liquid lunches, I wasn't surprised by her reaction. Everything was so twisted in this place that I expected that there wouldn't be much support for sobriety.

At least there was a Twelve-Step program brought in by two energetic guys in their mid-thirties, Santiago and Eric. Out of the 230 men in Beckham, only eight of them went to meetings, so it didn't take long to become chairperson of the group. My main motive for doing this was to get Eric and Santiago to take us to outside meetings at least once a week. This enabled me to meet people from all over Dade County so I could start setting up a support group for when I got out of prison.

I was looking forward to getting a job, but was disappointed when I found out that the private company running the joint took almost all your earnings. The profits for running Beckham came from the 45 percent of our paychecks that were kept for room and board. They put the other 55 percent in the bank and kept the interest. We were given a measly $30 a week draw and ate baloney and cheese sandwiches.

Before I could get a job I had to get an identification card. I was shocked when I was told to walk two blocks and then hop on the public bus to get to the licensing office. I couldn't believe that they would let me go off on my own like that and it made me a little nervous. As I walked out of the facility, I told myself that this was the time to prove to myself that I could make the right choices while in the real world. The first decision I made was to save $2.50 by skipping the bus and walking to the licensing center. Eight blocks later, I found myself standing on the sidewalk, looking across the street at a

Budweiser sign hanging in the window of a bodega. At the cross-roads, I had the little devil on my left shoulder saying, "Go ahead, buy a beer. You deserve it. You have five hours till you have to be back at Beckham, and if you have just one it will be out of your system by then." On my right shoulder, the little guy with the halo was saying, "Not a good idea. You've never had just one beer in your life."

Hearing the guy with the horns again shook me up—it was a long time since he'd popped in. I thought I had gotten rid of him. Somehow, I ignored him and kept walking. About a block up, I was greeted with the aroma of stale beer, tobacco, and vomit. When I looked around the corner, I saw a drunk using a squeegee on the sidewalk. A dive bar was hosing off the floors and letting the water run out into the streets, and the bum was trying to get to it before it went into the gutter. This time I didn't need the angel on my shoulder to tell me that this was where I could end up if I drank that one beer. I also knew that a higher power is what kept me from such a fate.

My involvement with the Twelve-Step program also helped me land my first job. Jimmy O'C. hooked me up with another guy in recovery who ran an advertising agency. Jimmy's buddy hired me for a customer service job. I worked under another recovering drug addict named Phil. For six bucks an hour, I was expected to show up in a shirt and tie and pretend that my name was Richard Clark. The fact that I wasn't supposed to use my real name was my first clue that something shady was going down. The second clue was hearing some of the other guys in customer service pretending to be bankers and lawyers.

The business wasn't really advertising; it was scamming small businesses into paying way too much for imprinted items like pens, coffee mugs, and so forth. We'd pull them in by telling them they won one of five gifts ranging from a print by Pacheco the Fight Doctor to a Lincoln Town Car. Our sales team would then sell them overpriced junk with their business name and number on them, and

we'd call it advertising. There was no such thing as quantity dis-
counts, so people would order 100 pens at $3.50 each and then end
up with a bill for $350. The day before the delivery, the customer ser-
vice reps would call to confirm that the customers were prepared to
pay COD. Not surprisingly, many people would balk at forking over
$350 for a small box of pens and would refuse to pay. That's when
the customer service reps would turn into bankers and lawyers.
When I voiced my concern about hurting people who really couldn't
afford spending this kind of money, I was told that if we didn't do it,
someone else would. For the first two weeks there, I told myself that
this job was probably the best I could do. Then I found out how
much it cost us to make one of those crappy pens: three and a half
cents! We were making a 1000 percent profit. Even though the scam
job was technically legal, I believed it was was a moral issue. Since I
had started working the steps, I was committed to always being honest; now I was getting paid to lie.

I desperately wanted out of the job, but the chief at Beckham had
told me that if I ever quit a job I'd be sent back to prison. If I was
fired, I might not be shipped back, but it depended on the circum-
stances. For the next eight weeks I was miserable. I dreaded spending my days lying and cheating innocent people.

By this time I'd become friendly with two corrections officers
who were sergeants, Tisha and Jamal. I told them about my dilemma
and they tried to get me to hang in there.

"You are so close to getting out now," Tisha tried to reason with
me. "Use your head. Just stick it out."

"But this makes me go against my new values system," I argued.

"You just need to make it through a little longer," Jamal assured me.

I listened to them for a while and then one day that was it. I
couldn't take it anymore and started telling customers not to waste
their money. At lunchtime I just left and started walking to the bus
stop to head back to Beckham and face the music. Before I got there,

Phil and another guy pulled up next to me in a Lincoln Town Car.

"Richard, where are you going?" Phil challenged me.

"I quit. I can't take this.. I'm heading back to the center," I said as I kept walking.

As the car rolled alongside me, Phil snapped. "After all we've done for you!" he shouted. "You lousy con, you're screwing *us* over!"

"Yep," was all I said.

Phil started to get out of the car to come after me as if he was going to beat my ass. I was hoping he would because I really wanted to lay him out.

"C'mon, Phil, calm down!" shouted his pal driving the car. "This piece of shit ain't worth it."

As Phil flipped me off and the car sped off down the street, I was filled with a strong sense of self-satisfaction. Although I wished I didn't want to beat the hell out of Phil, I was proud of myself for living up to my principle of being honest. I took the bus back to the center, but before I went in I called Bill from the pay phone on the corner. I filled him in on everything that happened.

"Well, I think you did the right thing," he agreed with me. After a long sigh, he added, "I just hope that you won't have to pay for it by going back to prison."

After hanging up, I returned to the center, signed in, and informed the guard at the front desk that I'd quit my job. He immediately hopped onto his phone, and I headed back to my room to start packing. Right before I got there, I ran into Jamal and told him what I had done and why. He immediately took off for the administration building.

Fifteen minutes later both Tisha and Jamal appeared in my doorway. "The chief was ready to ship your ass back to prison but we talked to him," Tisha said excitedly. "We told him that you left the job because you knew that there was fraud being perpetrated there."

I just looked at her blankly.

She continued, "We told the chief that it wouldn't have looked good for you to be caught in a raid by the Feds. Imagine the head-lines: *Work Release Inmate Caught In Sting.*"

"Yeah!" Jamal jumped in. "And we told him that you shouldn't be punished for doing the right thing."

"And?" I was afraid to hear what had happened.

"Unpack your bags!" they said in unison. "You're staying!"

With a sigh of relief I thanked them for having faith in me.

Since that day in 1990 I have always been given what I need as long as I do the right thing. I've always had a roof over my head, food in my belly, and the ability to make a living as long as I try to live by the principles I learned in the Twelve-Step program. Slowly but surely, I was becoming a better person. I was beginning to stop thinking just about myself and start thinking about other people.

Bill played a big role in this change. He would always talk about committing random acts of kindness. The first time he brought it up to me I pretended to stick my finger down my throat and throw up, but it wasn't long before he had me doing all sorts of things. I started tossing in extra change at the tollbooth to pay for the person behind me, and to put away cans that fell on the floor in the grocery store. He even got me to put change in the parking meter for a Mercedes that had run out of time. Of course, I griped about having to help out some rich bastard when I only brought home thirty bucks a week, but I still did it. After a while, I started doing this kind of crap out of habit. I didn't even need for Bill to get on my case. I wasn't perfect, but at least I was making progress.

Within a week of my dramatic departure from the world of advertising, I landed a job working for a French interior designer named Paulette. I was basically her boy Friday, and I spent much of my time cruising around in her VW Cabriolet running errands for her. I'd pick up materials, deliver samples, pay subcontractors, and drop off plans for future jobs. Although somewhat wary of me at first, Paulette ended up investing a lot of trust in me over time. During this time another Twelve-Step convention was held and my friend Eric showed up at the center asking if I wanted to attend. It was Saturday, the last day of the event, and a big dinner was being held that evening. Of course, you could do whatever you wanted at Beckham so it was no problem for me to go, and I brought another inmate from our inside program with me.

I was excited to be out on a Saturday night, and there were over 1,000 recovering addicts there that evening. As soon as we got there, Eric took off with his date. Since I didn't have dinner tickets, I just hung out in the lobby and bullshitted with a bunch of guys I knew from various outside meetings I attended. As we chatted away, I looked up and noticed a beautiful blonde walking down the ramp from the banquet rooms.

I knew that she had to be there for me. Just two days before I'd prayed to God for someone to love and I was very specific in my request. I asked for a woman between thirty-two and thirty-nine, between five feet, five inches tall and five feet, nine inches tall, with long blonde hair. As I said my prayer I envisioned this woman wearing a business pantsuit, walking with purpose, and filled with self-confidence. Oh, yeah, and since I couldn't help her with any money, she would be self-sufficient with a good job.

Now, here I was at the convention, and this woman who seemed to meet all my criteria was strutting in my direction. Not wanting to gawk, I returned to the conversation with the boys. About a minute later, I felt someone tapping me on the shoulder and it was my prayer come true.

"Is someone sitting here?" she smiled, pointing at the chair next to me.

"Uh, no," I mumbled. I was shocked because I never thought anyone this good looking would approach me. I forgot that I wasn't wearing a prison uniform and she had no way of knowing that I was a convict.

After a few seconds, she said, "Hi, my name is Faye."

"My name is Richard," I answered. I felt like an idiot—it was so long since I flirted with a woman, I didn't know what to say.

Somehow we got beyond the awkward introduction and ended up talking for two hours. I decided I should let her know up front about who and what I was, and she didn't skip a beat. She didn't care that I was a con—all she wanted was to get to know me.

When the dance started, we headed out onto the floor and didn't leave it until the night was over. Before leaving, I gave her my work number and she gave me her number at home. Eric got me back to the center before midnight, and as I lay in bed that night I looked forward to the future. The next day I put Faye on my visitation and furlough lists. It took a couple of weeks for them to check Faye out to make sure she wasn't Ma Barker. At the same time she was checking my story out to make sure that I wasn't a rapist or something more evil than being a killer. I passed her test and soon I was out on furloughs with her every weekend.

Things were going well with Faye, but they soon went sour with my boss, Paulette. After months of listening to her putting everything down in the United States, I got fed up. One day she was bragging about how easy it was for her to rip off her stupid American clients and I just couldn't take it. I told her that if it weren't for us stupid Americans she would probably be speaking German instead of French. The next day I was laid off.

Getting fired didn't send me back to prison, but I did need to find a new gig. I hit the jackpot when I scored a job at a ritzy hotel in Bal Harbour. Jeff, a friend of Bill's who was in the program, owned a catering company that was hired by the hotel to run the kitchen, dining room, inside bar, room service, and cabana service by the pool.

When I started in October, things were slow and I only worked the day shift. As soon as the tourist season kicked in I was working all sorts of hours. I would work room service in the mornings, play host in the afternoons, and bartend in the evenings. Beckham Hall didn't care how much I was working because the more money I made the more they took in.

The hotel was owned by a group of people from Washington, D.C., and Jeff had fifty-four bosses to answer to—and most of them were pains in the ass. It was high maintenance to say the least. The bosses were all influential in their own way; they ranged from presidential candidates to billionaires with the same last name as pharmaceutical companies. All of them seemed to do a lot of business by the pool.

It amazed me that a con like me would be allowed to work in a place where there were so many people on security detail. Somehow, I was always under the radar. When the Soviets and the East Germans were holding negotiations with the U.S., I was serving them breakfast. When the best-known supermodel ordered lunch and answered the door in her negligee, I delivered it to her. When the hotel hosted the Orange Bowl committee for New Year's Eve, I ran the party. There I was, amidst the most powerful people in the world, and I wasn't even an ex-con—I was still locked up! Although I had fleeting thoughts of creating an international incident from time to time, they were just that: fleeting. I simply kept myself amused by being the undercover con.

The more hours I put in at the hotel, the less I saw of Faye. It was nothing new for me to put work before anything else, but Faye didn't like it. Ironically, she also took issue with my lack of cash. Eventually our romance just fizzled away.

As our relationship came to an end so did my job. Jeff got tired of putting up with his fifty-four bosses and told them to find someone else to bitch at. This could have been a disaster for me because I was only a couple months away from my parole date, and I had to find another job. Luckily I landed one right away. It was working as a waiter in an old hotel on the beach, and it paid enough money to cover the $400 rent I would have once I got out.

I was seven and a half years sober, had worked the Twelve Steps, and thought I was ready to be in the real world full-time. There's an old saying: "If you want to give God a good laugh, tell him your plans." I was about to find out that the joke was on me.

Chapter Twenty-Eight

ABOUT A WEEK BEFORE MY RELEASE DATE, A PAROLE investigator paid me a visit. "Mr. Broom, I understand you're scheduled to be released next Thursday. I'm here to find out what your plans are and to let you know the guidelines you need to follow when you get out."

"Great, sir," I said. At this point, I didn't even really care what he was going to tell me, I was just so excited to finally reach the point where I was being prepped for release.

"Okay, well what are you planning on doing once you get out?" he asked, pen in hand, ready to scribble down my answer.

"Well, I am working at the old Shoreline Hotel as a waiter and plan to continue doing that. Other than working, I just plan on continuing my involvement with the Twelve-Step groups I've been attending."

"Good, good," he said, writing something down. "What about a place to live?"

"I found an apartment near the hotel."

"So it sounds like you are ready to go," he smiled.

"You better believe it!" I laughed.

"Alright, well I'm sure that you know you've got to keep your nose clean and stay out of trouble. Also, there's to be no contact with the victim's family."

"But I was hoping to let them know how sorry I am—"

"Not while you are on parole, Mr. Broom," he cut me off.

"But I just want to make my amends with them, and I was waiting to do that until I got out so they didn't think I was just doing it so they would get off my back with the parole commission."

"I'm sure you had the best of intentions," he said half-heartedly. "However, there is to be no contact with them. Understand?"

"Yes, sir," I replied. Although I was upset, I was also somewhat relieved that I was off the hook for a while longer. While I genuinely wanted to let the family know that I wished the shooting never happened, I was dreading facing up to it and hearing their response.

My release day came, April 4, 1991, thirteen days before my forty-fifth birthday. I spent the morning waiting around the center to be called up front to get my paperwork and find out where to meet my parole officer. It was the afternoon when I finally heard over the speaker system: "Richard Broom, please report to the sergeant's office."

As soon as I walked into his office, I knew something was wrong. He was sitting at his desk, flanked by four of the larger guards, with two on each side of him. There were never any guards there when you were about to be released. There was no need for them.

"I have some bad news, Richard. The parole commission has changed its mind and decided not to parole you today."

My mind went blank and all I could see was red.

"And," the sergeant continued, "since we believe you might run if you stick around here, we are sending you back to prison." Moments later, I was in shackles again.

My blood felt like it was on fire. Although I didn't show it, I was furious. All I kept thinking was that the first guard who gave me shit was going to have his larynx crushed by my fist. Somebody had to pay for this.

With my hands cuffed to my waist and ankle chains on, I hobbled back to my room to gather my few belongings. I was escorted out of the building to a van that would take me to Dade Correctional Institute. Knowing the ride would take about an hour, I did the only thing I could think of that might keep me from snapping: I started praying. Bill made me learn the third step prayer and I usually said it every morning. As I bounced around in the back of the van with my heart pounding and my brain feeling like it was about to explode, I closed my eyes and quietly said the following prayer:

"God, I offer myself to Thee—to build with me and to do with me as Thou wilt. Relieve me of the bondage of self, that I may better do Thy will. Take away my difficulties, that victory over them may bear witness to those I would help of Thy Power, Thy Love, and Thy Way of Life. May I do Thy will always."

It didn't work; it didn't calm me down, but I tried it again . . . and again and again. I must have said it at least fifty times during the ride.

As I repeated the prayer over and over, I kept thinking about what it meant to "take away my difficulties, that victory over them may bear witness to those I would help." I realized that it meant that my difficulties weren't going to go away, but if I accepted them as God's will, I'd get through them without doing something stupid. I didn't have to like what was happening, all I had to do was accept it and believe that there must be a reason for it. Maybe this was happening so I could have a chance to make peace with the victim's family. Maybe I was supposed to bear witness and show others in the prison what can happen with God in your life. Although I still wasn't religious (I had too many issues with authority to do that), I'd developed a sense of spirituality and it was something that I was ready to share with other people.

Somehow, praying frantically and recognizing that there must be some greater plan that brought me to the prison allowed me to cool off. By the time I pulled up in front of Dade, I wasn't happy, but I also wasn't homicidal.

Upon my arrival at Dade, I was greeted by Moose, a con I knew from my days at Raiford. "Yo, Broom! Broom!" he shouted across the yard. "Welcome back to the jungle, man. Ha! C'mon over to horti-culture once you get your shit. We've got fresh buck and some dyna-mite homegrown!"

I tried to wave him off to tell him I wasn't interested, but he wasn't taking no for an answer. He hustled over to the parade of prisoners I was in and cajoled me, "Come over and have a couple, man. You need to relax."

"No thanks," I tried to shrug him off. I knew that getting drunk wouldn't solve anything and the last thing I needed to do was to lose control when I was so pissed off. "I still go to that twelve-step shit."

Taking a step back, he argued, "Well, look at the good it did you. You're still back in the joint."

"But at least I was out in the real world for a little while," I shot back. I was in no mood for his crap. "Where the hell have you been?" I challenged him.

"Fuck you! I knew you were coming this morning," he snapped back and then walked away. The only way he could have known about that was by being on the take, which meant he was ratting out the other prisoners. No wonder he was able to be so blatant about the buck and pot in front of the guards. I was glad I blew him off because he probably would have narked me out anyway.

I can't honestly say that I wasn't tempted to just throw it all away and have a drink. I still couldn't believe that I worked so hard to prove myself and instead of going forward, I was going backward. In the past, I would have just gotten loaded or attacked someone physically—but that was when I thought I'd never be able to get things right. Most of my life I was trapped in a cycle of being called a piece of shit, then acting like one. First Big Bob made me feel like a fuckup, and I would act out. Then, because I was acting out, every other authority figure assumed I was a loser as well. I never realized that I could break that cycle until I went to Twelve-Step meetings and met other people who did. Hearing so many people's stories about overcoming unbelievable challenges gave me a sense of hope that I never felt before. Now, even though I was pissed off about being screwed, I was able to keep myself together because I knew that someday I would be free again.

When I finally spoke with my lawyer, he filled me in on why I wasn't released. "Well, Richard, you're not going to like this," said Steve. "Apparently, the parole commissioner felt that because you're an admitted alcoholic, you couldn't be trusted. Supposedly he has a drinking problem of his own and couldn't see himself ever committing the crime you committed. The bottom line is that he just doesn't want you out."

"So if I never admitted to having a problem I would have gotten out?" I asked, dumbfounded.

"Well," Steve sighed. "I guess so."

"Unbelievable!" I howled and threw my hands up in the air. "C'mon, that's bullshit and you know it. It's the commissioners trying to hold on to their jobs by keeping inmates that fall under the old sentencing guidelines."

After hesitating for a moment, Steve confirmed my assumption when he finally said, "You're too smart for your own good."

Back in October 1983, the sentencing guidelines for the State of Florida were changed for several reasons. One reason was because there was no conformity around the state. Someone committing the same exact crime could be sentenced to five years by a judge in Miami or to fifteen years by a judge in Clearwater. The other reason was that the parole commission wasn't releasing enough people and the prisons were becoming overcrowded. With the new guidelines, it became possible to abolish the parole people altogether. In my case, under the new sentencing guidelines, I would have received a maximum of seventeen years and would have been out in seven years and eight months without any supervision from parole. It was now eight years since the guidelines were put into place and the nine remaining board members were determined to hang on to their jobs. So they stopped releasing us scumbags who were sentenced before the new guidelines came out. Yep, I was stuck in prison because the commissioner didn't want to lose his $96,000-a-year salary.

I knew that this was what was going on and it could have made me real bitter, but I decided to just let it go. It was more important for me to hang on to my sanity. I just kept telling myself that if I continued to do the next right thing, I would always get what I needed and eventually be released.

Trying to make sense of it all, I decided that one of the reasons why I must have come back to prison was for me to have a chance to make amends with the victim's family. When I asked Stephen if it was okay to write to them, he said he would set it up with the victim's compensation board.

I began the four-page letter by explaining that I wanted to talk to them in person but the parole commission wouldn't let me. I then acknowledged that I was an alcoholic and when I killed Daniel, I was delusional, irrational, and hated life and the world. Daniel was simply at the wrong place at the wrong time when I finally lost it all. I wished it had never happened and that I could have taken his place. I told them about the way I was trying to live my life now even though I was still incarcerated and that I would never do something like that again. I also let them know that I wasn't sending them the letter so that they would get off my back with the parole commission, and I encouraged them to continue going to the hearings. I was simply trying to clean up my side of the street and wanted them to know that I was wrong.

It felt good to send off the letter. About six months later, I was forgiven by almost everyone in the family—Daniel's parents, girlfriend, two kids, four sisters, and seven of his brothers. The only one who wouldn't forgive me was his eighth brother. I wasn't looking for anything from them, I just wanted to do the right thing. Making amends is actually one of the Twelve Steps, and I was grateful for the opportunity to do it. I knew it was one of the primary reasons why fate brought me back behind bars.

Another reason I think I returned to prison was to bring the Twelve-Step program back to Dade. The inside sponsor who had run the program was a classification officer who had retired a couple months earlier, and no one else wanted to replace him. When I discovered that none of the eighteen classification officers or the nine psychologists were willing to step up to the plate, I reached for the mighty pen. Every day I wrote letters to them asking why there wasn't a program. In each and every letter I reminded them that the State of Florida's Department of Corrections mandates that there must be a program. I also asked what they were doing with the money that was supposed to go to the program. After relentlessly harassing them for a week, I was called up to administration and kindly asked to stop sending the requests. I was informed that the meetings would be reinstated immediately. I knew that the only reason why they were doing it was because copies of the letters were going into everyone's file, and the questions about mismanagement of funds could come back to haunt them. I didn't care. Having the program back was all that mattered.

I discovered the third reason why I must have been sent back to the joint after my second Twelve-Step meeting. While talking with eight cons I knew from back in Raiford, I found out that they had no intention of going to meetings once they got out. When I asked them why, they told me that the people in the outside program didn't want them there.

"Listen, don't you know that 95 percent of the members don't care where you come from? " I argued. "And as far as the other 5 percent are concerned, they aren't living by the principles outlined in the Twelve Steps and Twelve Traditions."

"What do you mean?" asked one of the cons.

"The entire purpose of the program is to stay sober and to help another alcoholic do the same. The only requirement for membership is the desire not to drink," I pointed out. "If you really want to stay sober, you need to keep connected to the network. Remember, there's power in numbers. It's always easier when you have people around you who are trying to do the same thing you are."

I knew they were probably giving themselves an excuse not to go, but I felt it was up to me to take that excuse away from them. If it helped just one of them to succeed once he got out, it would be worth it. I was determined to make my time in prison matter, and getting these guys to outside meetings seemed like a noble cause.

After four months of prison life, Dade's superintendent asked me whether or not I would run if I went back to work release. Hearing me answer "no" was enough proof for him to ship me off to Beckham Hall a couple days later. This time it was no longer a testing ground for temptation. I'd already proven myself over and over again. While I realized I had to take it one day at a time, I was confident that I knew how to create a routine that would keep me out of trouble. The top priority was to get to meetings, and that wasn't a problem at Beckham.

The challenge this time was getting a job. I thought I could just pick up where I left off at the hotel, but there was a change in management and they didn't want me working there. Whenever I would fill out applications for other jobs and was asked if I've been arrested for, or convicted of, a felony in the last five years, I could honestly say no even though I was still locked up—but no one would hire me anyway. I came to the conclusion that I would have to get something through someone I knew, and, yet again, one of my contacts from the program came through for me. Eric, who ran the group at Beckham, ended up hiring me to work for his flooring company. He gave me a van to drive and I spent my days delivering carpets all over Miami. With my own transportation, I was able to make it to ten meetings a week and only three or four of them were sanctioned. I found a way to work faster and smarter so I could squeeze in meetings between deliveries. I wasn't doing this to get away with anything, I just wanted to get into the lifestyle of someone in recovery and set myself up for a successful life after prison.

In the late fall of 1991 I had to move yet again. Beckham Hall was shut down after the State Department of Corrections discovered that there was a lot of money missing—six figures worth! That wasn't the only reason the place collapsed, though. One of the inmates who was paying off the night guards in order to sneak out got into a drunk driving accident with his wife at two in the morning. I guess no one was following the rules around there.

When I found out I was going back to Miami North I was afraid they weren't going to let me keep the van. Fortunately, the chief let me hang on to it so I could keep working for Eric. It drove my old pal Officer Kumin up the wall though because he thought I was getting special treatment. As a result, he would shake me down every night when I came back to the center because he was determined to catch me doing something wrong.

Unfortunately, Eric relapsed shortly after my transfer. He started out on Jamaican beer and ended up on crack cocaine. His fall from favor was done in flamboyant fashion: he robbed his own business to the point where it went bankrupt. Even his father couldn't save it.

I spent my last days there working with a bunch of homeless guys as we helped Eric's family clean out the warehouse and move the remaining rugs back to their house.

Throughout the cleanup Eric's family was paying us cash everyday. One evening we were all getting on the bus and one of the homeless men had a ten-dollar bill, which the bus driver refused to break. To help the guy out so he wouldn't have to walk a half mile up the road to get change, I gave the guy two fives for his ten.

One of the rules of the work release center was that we were never supposed to have anything on us larger than a five-dollar bill, so I planned to break the ten-spot before I returned to the work release center. When our bus arrived late, I raced back to the center forgetting about the ten-dollar bill. As usual, Officer Kumin was waiting for me and when he found the larger bill on me, he tried to make a federal case out of it. The jerk-off refused to believe my explanation and was elated to hit me with the first disciplinary report I had received in ten years of incarceration. I had a hearing the following week, and my furlough was pulled for the following two weekends. The punishment didn't bother me, just the fact that the peckerhead was getting off on busting me for helping a poor homeless guy.

His crap wasn't going to stop me from continuing to commit my random acts of kindness, though. Bill would have busted my chops over it. He was determined to build my character. On top of this nice guy crap, he also had me asking myself four questions every night and writing the answers down to the first three in a journal. The first question was: "What did you do today that you respect yourself for?" The second question was: "What did you do for someone else today whether they knew it or not?" The third one was: "What did you enjoy today that had nothing to do with you?" The fourth one, which was the easiest for me to answer, was: "What bothered you today?" I had no problem coming up with things that pissed me off every day. The first three questions were much harder because in order for me to answer them I had to do something I wasn't used to doing. That's exactly what the exercise was all about: changing my habitual reactions to life.

When he first told me to do this, I asked him for an example of what I could do to respect myself.

"Well," he grinned as if he knew he was going to get me riled up. "You could stop giving the guards a hard time—even Kumin."

"What the hell are you talking about?" I asked incredulously. "That asshole is always giving me a hard time!"

"I know he's after you," he laughed. "But I hear you putting him down—and other people—all the time. Sometimes I don't think you even realize it. Essentially you call him an asshole without even saying the word. You've been locked up for a long time and you know how far you can go without getting written up."

I kept my mouth shut because I knew he was right.

"You have comebacks for everything," he continued. "You may not know this, but you are doing it to fuel your ego. Putting them down is your way of proving to yourself that you are smarter than them. Believe me, you don't need to build up your ego—you need to deflate it."

"So I'm supposed to think I'm just a piece of shit?" I jumped up.

"No, no, no. That's not what I'm saying." Realizing he touched a nerve, he tried to calm me down. "You need to build up your self-esteem rather than your ego."

"What's the freakin' difference?" I grumbled as I sat back down.

"Your ego is what you want people to think you are; your self-esteem is what you know you are. It's what you believe about yourself deep down inside. Remember what they say in meetings: alcoholics are egomaniacs with an inferiority complex."

"Okay, I can understand that. So how am I supposed to 'build my self-esteem'?" I asked, making quote signs in the air.

"Start accomplishing things, like keeping your mouth shut when Kumin starts giving you crap," Bill chuckled.

"And how can I do that?" I groaned.

"When Kumin gives you an opening, don't say a thing. Before you open your mouth think it through. Think and act, don't react. If you can force yourself to do this, you'll have something to write down that you respect yourself for."

"Yeah, I'll do that," I said sarcastically, even though I planned to try it.

"Good," he said, without acknowledging my attitude—he was used to it by now. "And every night before you go to bed, think about your day and come up with an event to satisfy question number one."

"Okay," I answered in a nicer tone. It was time to give the poor guy a break.

While question one was a bit of a challenge, question two was easy. I'd been doing random acts of kindness for a while now. And having to write something down every night forced me to be a decent human being at least once a day. I was still cleaning up spills in the supermarket, putting change in the parking meters, holding the door open for people twenty feet behind me, and all that kind of crap. I had no problem writing down something in my book every night—in fact, I usually had a couple entries.

For question number three, I had to enjoy something that had nothing to do with me, so I began watching the sunrise and sunset. Sometimes I'd pull over to watch a cool cloud formation. Other times I would just pause to listen to the birds or the sounds of children laughing. In order to having something to write down, I had to force myself to stop and smell the roses.

I showed Bill the journal entries every couple of weeks. After about six months of doing this, Bill told me to go back and read the entries from the first month, so I did. He then asked me if I remembered all the incidents that bothered me and what exactly had happened that made me so upset. To my surprise, I couldn't remember what happened that made me write it down so vigorously.

After reporting back to Bill on this, he posed the big question: "When you wrote down what bothered you, were you angry?"

"Of course I was angry," I answered.

"So it bothered you a lot, but you can't remember it, can you?" he continued to press the issue.

"No," I replied, wondering where he was going with this.

"Then why can't you remember the event?"

"I don't know," I started to get impatient.

Turning it all around, he pointed out, "So how important was it really?"

He got me there. I didn't answer him, but I got the message. It couldn't have been that important if I couldn't recall the problem five or six months later.

"Just keep in mind that most people get upset over life's ups and downs, but most of those ups and downs are just temporary—they exist for only a moment or two. They don't have a real effect on your life."

Since that day, whenever life's little problems pop up, I've asked myself, "How important is this, really, in the scheme of things? How important is this compared to the other difficulties in the world?" When I do this, I have fewer things troubling me. I find myself worrying less and enjoying my life more.

Bill also asked me that day if I noticed anything about my answers to the first three questions.

"Sure. I'm noticing more and more events that I respect myself for, and I spend a lot more time appreciating nature. I also spend less time listening to the committee in my head."

Bill patted me on the back. "You're changing, Richard. You're changing your reactions to life."

"How will I know that I'm getting better?" I asked.

"In your case," he grinned, "When someone yells 'asshole' and you don't look up."

Chapter Twenty-Nine

MY NEW RELEASE DATE WAS SCHEDULED FOR March 9, 1993. I spent the six months leading up to it romancing my latest lady friend, Meg, and working for another flooring company that was super busy in the cleanup after Hurricane Andrew. I also started every morning with prayers and meditation, and then tried to squeeze as many meetings in as I could. I always ended my day by answering the four questions and saying some more prayers.

As release day approached, I became more and more anxious. Afraid that I might be jerked around again, I tried to prepare myself for disappointment. Yet, I couldn't help feeling excited about the possibility of starting my new life. My plan was to keep my current job, live with Meg, and get more involved in the Twelve-Step program. Hopeful and happy, I was looking forward to being sober and free.

The day before I was supposed to get out, Mrs. V. from Miami North approached me. "Hi, Richard. So you're scheduled to get out tomorrow."

"Yep, I'll believe it when I see it, though," I quipped nervously, hoping she wasn't going to give me bad news.

"I just wanted to wish you good luck. I hope you have a good life," she said kindly. Then, out of nowhere, she asked, "So are you still going to the 5:30 meeting at New Horizon?"

My stomach immediately started churning. That was one of the meetings I was sneaking off to, so she obviously found out what I was up to. *Great,* I thought to myself. *I'm gonna get screwed again for going to too many meetings.* I tried not to panic and instead calmly asked, "How did you know about that?"

"My son told me he saw you there. I hope you keep going to them," she explained, reassuring me that my secret was safe with her. Apparently she'd known for a while and never ratted me out because she understood that going to those meetings would keep me out of prison.

After all the anticipation of imminent disaster, the morning of March 9 arrived, and I was released back into the world without any fireworks or fanfare. I entered a quiet office, signed a couple papers, walked out of the release center, and suddenly I was a free man. Meg was waiting outside and took me over to meet my parole officer. A calm, collected black woman in her late thirties, the officer just told me to follow the rules, keep a job, and pay my monthly fees. She also urged me to stay out of trouble, avoid drugs and alcohol, and never have a weapon.

Meg and I zipped over to a meeting right away. Arriving early for a change, I had time to chat with some of the regulars, including Boo, an ex-lieutenant in the department of corrections. When she found out about my release, she told me that I was one of the people she was keeping an eye on at the state convention back in 1989. She noticed that she never saw a smile on my face back then, and she was happy to see that things had changed. It was then that it hit me that I was really free.

That night, I didn't have to race back to the work release center to check in by 7:00 PM. We went out for prime rib instead—and I savored every bite of it. Afterward, we went to another meeting and then went home to Meg's condo where there were no guards, no cons, and no curfews.

By now I was a pro at setting up a new routine, and I knew how important that was going to be to ensure my successful transition. Staying busy seemed to keep me out of trouble, so I crammed as much into each day as I could. From work to meetings to the gym to more meetings—my schedule was always full. I tried to make time for Meg by taking her to a restaurant called My Father's Mustache every Friday night.

One evening in the restaurant, I almost choked on a meatball when I noticed Sergeant March stuffing his face in the nonsmoking section across from us. My immediate reaction was to storm over and bitch slap him. He had ruined so many cons' lives, and here he was living large, shoveling spaghetti in his mouth as if someone was going to take it away from him.

"You see that fatso in the yellow shirt?" I growled to Meg, nodding in March's direction.

"What about him?" Meg asked nervously. She had never saw seen me so angry.

"I want to go over to his table and knock him out"

"Why?" she asked after putting her hand on my knee to calm me down.

After telling her about how horrible he was, she begged me not to do anything. I didn't. Venting to her helped me cool off and stay rational. All my years in the program, in Go-Lab, and in all the other behavioral modification programs taught me that sharing your emotions was the best way to keep from acting on them. Still, sometimes that was hard to do when I was facing someone who had caused so much misery for so many people.

As I started to calm down, my tunnel vision opened up and I was able to see more clearly. I began to study March and realized that he was the one getting put down now. There he sat, slumped over his food, looking defeated, as the two women on either side of him chewed him out. Suddenly, I let out a hearty laugh.

Thinking that I had finally lost it, Meg asked, "Now what?"

"Look at how miserable he looks. I was just thinking about how I used to pray that he would go to heaven, but it looks like he ended up in a living hell!"

On the ride home, I kept thinking about how March seemed to get what he deserved. It was proof that you didn't have to get even with anyone; karma would take care of that. Certainly, I'd faced my own karma over the years and witnessed many other people facing theirs. I wished I'd remembered that before letting myself get so angry. I concluded that I wasn't perfect, but at least I was aware of my anger. I was finally managing my anger rather than letting it manage me. I also knew that if I started drinking again all of that would go out the window. It was yet one more reason to stay sober and continue going to meetings.

As time went on, it became obvious to me that although I liked Meg, I was never going to be in love with her. I probably never was going to meet someone who made me feel like a school boy again— those days were over. But I wasn't ready to settle either. Meg was a smart, sexy woman, but I wasn't as happy as I thought I'd be. When I tried to talk to her like a grown-up and tell her how I felt, she asked me to give us more time.

While I agreed to stick it out with her for a while, I decided that I needed to find a job that would pay enough for me to live on my own. At first I took a job at a car dealership, but left there as soon as I felt that I needed to be dishonest to make a sale. Then Bill kept me busy overseeing the renovation of his condo. Once that was complete, I worked for my old high school pal, Mickey, who was coordi-

nating conventions targeting the computer and electronics indus-
tries. My job was to call companies across North America to find out
who was in charge so we could invite them to an upcoming convention in Arizona. It was a temp job, so nine weeks later I was back in
the job hunt. I ended up working as a manager at a new restaurant
on Key Largo.

One evening while driving home after working a fourteen-hour
day at the restaurant, I was bitching to myself about having to commute over a hundred miles a day. *If only I spoke Spanish, then I could
get a damn job in Miami,* I groaned to myself. *But no, I have to drive
in this tiny fucking car, scrunched up like a sardine.* As I traveled
down the road with a pity party in my head, I noticed a straight line
of lights off in the distance. I didn't remember an airstrip being
there and, for a moment, wondered what the lights could be. I
quickly returned to complaining about the Cubans running Miami,
and my legs being cramped. When I got closer to the lights, I realized that they were actually in the shape of an oval. For the life of
me, I couldn't figure out what I was looking at until I came across a
sign that said Dade County Correctional Facility.

At that moment, I felt as if I was getting a spiritual smack-down.
Here I was, pissing and moaning about my commute, when fourteen
months ago I would have walked a hundred miles to work if they
had just let me out of the joint. Thanks to this much needed reality
check, I remembered to be grateful for everything I had: my sobriety, my job, my car, and my freedom.

For the rest of the ride home I kept thinking about other things I
could be thankful for and even decided that I should appreciate the
Cuban Americans who made Miami such a bustling city. If I was
really supposed to work there, I would. Apparently, it was in the stars
for me to return to Miami. Not long after that evening, the restaurant slowed down and I ended up getting a sales job back in the city
working with a company that placed Occupational Safety and

Health Administration (OSHA) compliance and Drug-Free Work-place Programs in small businesses.

About the same time I left my restaurant job, I found a way to get tossed out of Meg's apartment. I boogied the night away at a Twelve-Step clubhouse dance and then went to breakfast with a bunch of people, including a sassy senorita, then showed up at the condo at 3:00 AM. When Meg confronted me and asked me point-blank if I was with someone, I answered, "Yes." I wasn't with the senorita in the biblical sense, but I did spend much of the evening hitting on her. Meg assumed I was out getting laid—even though I wasn't—but I didn't tell her any differently. There was no question that it was the end of the line for us anyway, so I just used the blowup as a way out.

In my time of crisis, I did what every good Twelve-Stepper does, I called my sponsor. As usual, Bill came through for me. Ironically, the same day Meg kicked me out Bill found out about a Lutheran church that needed a groundskeeper. In exchange for opening and closing the building for meetings and mowing the lawn once a week, I was allowed to live for free in the apartment on-site—and almost all my utilities were included. For the first time in my life, I was living alone. If I wanted to be around people, I could go to the Twelve-Step clubhouse or a meeting. When I wanted to be on my own, I could just stay home. After all the years of being forced to deal with cons and guards in my face around the clock, time alone was a luxury.

My biggest challenge at this point was trying to figure out where I belonged professionally. I tried my best at the OSHA compliance company, but it just didn't pay enough. I hopped around from job to job after that, first selling security equipment then water treat-ment equipment. I worked at two different water treatment compa-nies. I had to leave the first one because the management there kept pressuring me to lie. Their competitor actually called me out of the blue to hire me after they heard that I refused to be dishonest. Again, doing the right thing paid off, but I still wondered if sales was really where I belonged. I decided to stick it out for the time being as it was paying the bills.

In the spring of 1995 I found out I was being hired for one of the most important jobs of my life: walking my daughter Katie down the aisle. Her wedding was scheduled for July 15 at an old Presbyterian church in Troy, New York. I was elated that she wanted me to be a part of the wedding. Her plan was to split the fatherly duties between her stepdad, Mike, and me. I would be part of her ceremony, and Mike would have the first dance.

Five days before the big event, I flew into Albany to participate in all the prewedding hoopla. I bonded with the boys by picking up my tux; playing golf with the groom, his best man, and Big Bob; and even going to the bachelor party. The night of the rehearsal I finally saw my younger daughter, Erin, for the first time in fourteen and a half years. Although we'd spoken a couple times, she didn't really know me, so I wasn't surprised when she was standoffish.

The wedding was beautiful, as was Katie. Before I escorted her down the aisle, I asked Erin to fix my tie. I didn't really need her to; I just wanted to share a moment with her.

The ceremony went off without a hitch and all 150 guests celebrated at a giant banquet hall in North Troy. It was a trip down memory lane: not only were both my ex-wives there, but so were a load of family members and countless old friends. I also made a new friend that night. My daughter's nutritionist, Harmony, and I took a couple spins around the dance floor.

About halfway through the reception, I toasted the married couple with a champagne glass filled with club soda. I could tell that more than a couple people were wondering what was in my glass. Realizing that there were a lot of people there who were negatively affected by my years of drinking, I began to think that maybe it was time to move back to New York to make my amends.

The morning after, I woke up to the phone ringing. It was David, the father of my fraternity brother Josh. According to David, Josh was struggling with alcohol and needed help. Harmony was by my side when I got the call and came along with me. She was in the program as well, and you were supposed to have two recovering people when making this type of call. When we arrived at Josh's, he was lounging on the couch in a pair of shorts. I immediately noticed that one of his legs was dark blue and purple, and swollen to about twice its normal size. His other leg was red and a bit swollen, as well. These were telltale signs that his liver wasn't functioning and I knew that getting him off the booze was a matter of life or death.

After some brief chitchat, Harmony excused herself to the kitchen to go talk with David and Josh's mom. Josh and I started reminiscing about the good old days when we first started partying in the fraternity. After some laughs, I knew it was time to cut to the chase. "You know, I used to think that booze was a magic potion, but look where it got me. It's really just a poison."

Josh seemed receptive to my observation and I took that as an opening to get him talking about his own battle with booze. We talked for almost four hours and by the end of our conversation, he'd decided to start going to a Twelve-Step program. I also made my amends with Josh for giving him a wicked beating in a bar years earlier.

As I left his home, I thought about all the messes I needed to clean up in New York and decided I was going to find a way to have my parole transferred back up to Albany. I didn't know how long it was going to take, but knew it was time to go home.

Upon my return to Miami, I sprang into action. I immediately started the paperwork to apply for my parole to be switched up to New York. My plan was to live with Harmony and be her assistant by helping to sell a natural product called "super blue algae." I was also going to work for the Albany distributor of the water treatment company I was working for in Florida.

The drive up the coast was quite different from those when I was working for Fritz. Going five miles over the speed limit wasn't an issue since I didn't have 350 pounds of pot in the car. No longer paranoid about being busted, I even went across the Delaware Bridge and took the New Jersey Turnpike rather than cutting through Pennsylvania. It was a much more enjoyable ride.

It didn't take long for all my plans to change once I got to New York. Harmony ended up being a handful. It wasn't long before I was flying solo again.

Luckily, I decided not to live with her when I returned to New York. It seemed like it was the right time to show Mom and Big Bob that I had finally got my act together, so I moved in with them instead. As empty nesters, they had a couple bedrooms for me to stay in, but I still opted for the basement. I knew I would probably only be there for a year. My intention was to stay in New York until I made all my amends, and then I was going to return to Miami.

When I went to my first meeting after moving back, I ran into my old fraternity brother Butch. He was working as a counselor in a treatment facility just west of Schenectady. He also had his own business where he would find addicts for treatment facilities by getting referrals from various unions in New York and Massachusetts. Not long after we reconnected, he hooked me up with a job interview with a woman named Jan at a treatment center called the Pines. It wasn't a counseling job; it was more like being a babysitter. But I was expected to talk about the program and help patients work toward sobriety. After sponsoring a lot of guys in the Twelve-Step program, teaching in Go-Lab, and running some other behavioral modification programs, I figured it might be a good match for me.

I was all charged up for the job until I walked into the treatment center and saw a bunch of the patients stagger by. Heavily medicated, they reminded me of the cons who were pumped up with Thorazine so that they would behave in prison. *To hell with this,* I thought to myself. I wanted to just leave but didn't want to screw Butch. He had put himself out to help me, and when you're an ex-con, you don't shit on people who try to help you. As I waited for Jan, I decided that I could get out of the job by sabotaging the interview. All I had to do was to let her know who I was and where I came from.

Moments later a short, energetic woman came bounding into the front office. As she shook my hand, she cheerfully introduced herself. "Hello! You must be Richard Broom. It's a pleasure to meet you! I'm Jan Larson."

"Yes, nice to meet you, too," I mumbled. Trying to nip this in the bud, I blurted out, "I want you to know something, so I don't waste too much of your time."

"Sure, what is it, dear?" she asked, still grinning from ear to ear. Damn, she was just a bundle of sunshine!

"I spent eleven years in prison for murder," I declared, placing the emphasis on the word murder.

"Gooood!" she exclaimed. "There are a lot of men on the second floor unit who have legal problems. You'll be perfect for the second shift!"

Before I knew it, I was getting the grand tour and introduced as a new staff member without even officially accepting the job. While I didn't really want it, I couldn't turn it down. It made sense that I would wind up working in the recovery field. After everything I'd been through, it was where I belonged. Plus, it was one career where you didn't get ahead by lying. You succeeded by sharing the truth.

I was at a point in my life where it was time to honestly face up to my past. Years earlier, when working the eighth step, I had put together a list of all the people I needed to make amends to; Mom and Big Bob were on the top of the list. Living with them gave me the chance to mend our relationship. I'd forgiven them years ago for everything they put me through, but I was now mature enough to realize that I had caused them a great amount of grief as well. We didn't really talk about everything that happened, but spending a year together and showing them that I was sober, stable, and hardworking gave them the peace of mind that they needed and deserved.

It was different when it came to my two daughters. With Kate, I admitted to being an asshole and running away from my responsibilities in 1980. I tried to spend as much time as I could with her while I was living in New York without becoming a nuisance. Kate and I already had a good relationship, so it was much easier with her than it was with Erin.

I never had a chance to build a relationship with Erin; I was gone so soon after she was born. I tried to make my amends by being there without interfering with her life. She was working at an ice cream shop, and I'd go visit her there once every couple of weeks. I'd just go in, order a cone, and try to make small talk with her. While Erin never said anything to me about it, Debbie eventually called me and told me to stop visiting her because I was making her uncomfortable. I wasn't sure if I should believe Debbie, as I knew she was still the consummate drama queen, but I backed off anyway. Erin already had a father: her stepfather, Barry. She didn't need me. I just wanted her to know that I would be there for her, but it may have been too late.

Making amends with my two ex-wives wasn't altogether easy either. I spent more time listening to them than talking to them. They both still needed to vent and remind me what a bastard I was. I don't think either of them wanted to hear what I had to say. Each time I tried to talk to them, they would just tell me, "You'll never change." It didn't bother me because I knew who I had become and how hard I'd worked to get to where I was. I wasn't worried about what other people thought about me anymore. I knew I was a decent human being doing the right thing.

In order to make amends to many of the people on my list, I had to visit a bunch of my old haunts to hunt them down. I found some folks right away and got leads on others. When I had time, I would call around to find the rest. With all the hell I'd raised over the years, it was quite an undertaking, but I kept plugging away.

Since arriving back in New York, I went to a bunch of meetings with my frat brother Josh. He seemed to be doing fairly well since the intervention the day after Kate's wedding. In early November, I asked him several times to go to a meeting with me and each time he came up with an excuse not to go. On Thanksgiving, I got a drunken call from him.

"Hey, Richard," he slurred. "Happy Turkey Day!"

"Yeah, Josh. Happy Thanksgiving. Sounds like you've had more than turkey today," I replied.

"Oh, well, I'm only drinking on the holidays," he tried to explain.

"Most alcoholics can't just drink on the holidays, Josh." I wasn't going to let him off the hook.

Realizing that I was calling him on his bullshit, he tried to change the subject. "So, my mom . . . whoops!" he said as he dropped the phone. After recovering it, he continued, "Well my mom said that she doesn't want me going to any meetings anymore. She said it was embarrassing."

I wanted to ask him if his mom thought the neighbors wouldn't have something to say about him crawling onto the front porch at six in the morning. Instead, I asked him, "Why do you think it's okay to try to kill yourself on a holiday?"

"Don't worry, brother, I'm just celebrating," he answered cheerfully.

"C'mon, Josh. Cut the bullshit," I tried to confront him.

"Okay, man. Have a Happy Turkey Day!" he said as he hung up the phone.

I was worried, but had to let it go and hope for the best. On Christmas Day, we had the same conversation, then again on New Year's Eve and New Year's Day. In the middle of January he called, wasted again. When I asked him what holiday it was he told me, "It's the feast of Saint Agnes. How could you not know that?" he laughed.

"Gee, I don't know," I replied sarcastically.

"Listen, I have a Catholic saints calendar and a couple others, and it winds up that every day is a holiday!" he laughed again. He was sounding more and more pathetic as the conversation went on.

"I'm sorry to hear you feel that way. Call me once you've had your fill of booze," I sadly said, then hung up the phone.

During the second week of March, David called me. "You lost a good friend today, Richard."

"What?" I asked, not yet comprehending what he was saying.

"Josh passed away," he explained, beginning to get choked up.

"How the hell did that happen?" I asked, although I knew the answer.

"His liver stopped working and then his kidneys failed," David cried. "I told him to keep fighting, but he just gave up."

"I'm sorry to hear that, David."

"You were such a good friend and really tried to help him." David began to pull himself together. "We wanted to know if you would be a pallbearer at the funeral."

I refused, telling him I was starting a new job that day. The real reason was that I was afraid I might go off on Josh's mother. I was furious with her for asking Josh to stop going to meetings because she thought it didn't look good for the family. I wanted to ask her if she still cared about what the neighbors thought. Yet, as much as I wanted to blame her, I knew it was Josh's fault. He's the one who had picked up the drink. He'd killed himself. The tragedy made me even more determined to stay sober.

My excuse for not going to the funeral was actually true. Butch hired me to drive addicts to a rehab called Kinderhook Lodge, a small facility in a secluded area near Kingston. Most of the people I was picking up were in New York City, but occasionally I went to Binghamton, Syracuse, New Jersey, and even Boston. The people I picked up were referred to us by their union reps and in many cases, they had to clean themselves up to save their jobs. As I drove around picking them up, it reminded me of the old days when I was making collections for Joe, except now I was collecting lives and souls.

I liked the job because every day there was a different challenge. I got to know how to get around New York City really well. Butch was working with the restaurant and transit authority unions, so they had people in all five boroughs. I was picking up lost souls everywhere, from Harlem to Greenwich Village to the projects in Brooklyn.

One time I went to Long Island City to pick up a woman working for the transit authority. I showed up at her mother's apartment at 2:00 PM, the time we had scheduled, and she was nowhere to be found. I could tell by the look in her mother's eyes that she was worried. "Please wait for her. She'll be home soon," she pleaded.

So I waited, and waited, and waited. Hours later, I got on the pay phone across the street to call her union handlers to find out what they wanted me to do.

"Fuck her if she isn't there," they told me. "Just leave."

I went back up to the apartment one more time and her mom begged me to stay. Seeing her desperation, I stuck around for another two hours. I was getting anxious because it was now after dark. Right as I was ready to leave, her daughter showed up high on crack cocaine. I was able to get her into the car and tried to give her advice on the ride up to the rehab. I told her to hang out with the patients who talked the same way in private as they did in front of the group. I encouraged her to stick with the winners and reminded her that her job was at stake. When I finally dropped her off, I was doubtful that she was going to follow any of my advice. A couple of weeks later I found out that she was sent home because she gave the whole place the crabs.

While it was often a struggle to bring people in, sometimes it was worth it—take James, for example. He was a sixty-year-old dishwasher in Harlem who was about to retire from a hotel he had worked at for twenty-five years. According to his union rep, the hotel was trying to fire him because he was drinking on the job. The truth was that he had been drinking on the job for the twenty-five years he worked there and it was overlooked, but now it was being used as an excuse to screw him out of his pension.

The pickup time was scheduled for 1:00 PM. While driving around his block trying to find a parking spot, I passed his building and saw seven men and women sitting in lawn chairs out front, all of them sipping out of bottles in brown paper bags. Once I parked the car, I went to the pay phone to call James to make sure he was ready to go. His sister answered the phone and said he was downstairs. When I told her who I was, she said with a sense of urgency, "Hold on! I'll go get him."

I sat there on the pay phone waiting for ten minutes until James finally got on the phone. "Are you ready?" I asked. "I'm around the corner on a pay phone."

"What? You ain't supposed to be here till four o'clock!" he claimed.

"James, I told you one o'clock," I said firmly. I knew what he was up to; he was trying to cling to his old lifestyle for as long as he could.

"No, four o'clock!" he argued.

"James, I haven't had a drink in thirteen years, and it's real clear to me what I said. It was one o'clock. Are you ready? Did you pack?" I asked, already knowing his answer.

"No," he answered.

"Be ready in fifteen minutes. I'll pull up in front. Since I can't park, be ready," I ordered him.

James began to stammer about "fo' o'clock" and I cut him off. "If you aren't ready, I'll leave you here," I warned him. "I hate to see you lose your pension, but I'm not going to fuck around all afternoon, so be ready." I hung up the phone and James was on the clock.

After about twenty minutes of hanging on the corner in Harlem, I got into my car and pulled up in front of James's place. A small thin man carrying a suitcase slowly walked up to my car. I got out and helped him put his bag in my trunk.

"Should I sit in the back?" he asked shyly.

"I think you'll be more comfortable up front," I told him.

As we were about to leave, two of James's drinking buddies stumbled over to the car. I immediately thought of Sanford and Son because they looked just like Bubba and Grady. Grady was completely wasted and was wearing a bus driver's uniform. I wondered if he was just coming from or about to go to work.

"Where you takin' James?" Grady demanded.

"You don't need to know," I tried to brush him off.

Bubba didn't seem to appreciate my attitude and asked again, "We said, where you takin' James?"

"All you need to know is that I'm not a cop and he isn't going to jail," I said, trying to calm them down.

Seeing them glaring at me as if they were ready to pounce, James jumped in. "It's okay, it's okay, man. He's taking me to an alcohol rehab."

The boys immediately backed off. "Good for you, James," they said. "That'll be good for you." For some reason, I believed they really meant it.

When we got to Kinderhook, I hung out with James while he was getting checked in. His nurse informed me that his blood alcohol level was .37—which was close to dead. It must have been even higher when I picked him up two hours earlier. I wondered what would have happened if I'd given him until four o'clock.

James had to go the hospital for a while, but then returned to Kinderhook. I checked in on him regularly while he was there. When his month was up, I drove him home. On the ride back I tried to share every bit of pearly wisdom I could. I told him about the Twelve Steps and why he needed to do them. I could tell that he was a changed man.

"Yeah, I'm feelin' good now. It's been a long time since I felt this way. Now I can enjoy my retirement," he smiled as he looked out the window.

"That's right, James. What are you planning on doing with all that time?" I asked, hoping he was going to stay busy enough to keep himself out of trouble.

"I'm headin' down to Mississippi and Tennessee to visit family."

"Have you been down there before?"

"Yeah, but I don't remember any of it. This time I'll be able to take in all the scenery and enjoy the ride."

Hearing the hope in his voice made me beam. As we pulled up in front of his apartment building, I wished him good luck.

He leaned over, shook my hand, and said, "Thanks for not leaving me behind a month ago." As I watched him walk away, I knew that he was going to succeed. The fact that he was willing to let his drinking buddies know what he was doing showed me that he was ready to change. It was another miracle, and I was grateful to play a part in it.

Chapter Thirty

I'D BEEN IN NEW YORK FOR OVER A YEAR WHEN I RAN into two old friends of mine at my Monday night bowling league. Ray and Eddie were pals of mine since elementary school and Ray was my best man at my second wedding. They heard I was in town from Ray's brother Gary, who was in my league, and decided to pop in to catch up on old times. Sitting in the lounge, they both ordered beers and I asked for a club soda.

"What the hell are you doing, Dick?" Ray started busting on me. "I thought I could count on you to toss down a couple with us!"

"I'm not drinking anymore, Ray—and I don't go by Dick these days either," I said seriously. "Call me Richard, okay?"

"Don't tell me you're no fun anymore!" Ray pressed. "Where's the guy who would dance on the tables and make smartass comments to innocent victims walking by?"

"Yeah, we were looking forward to seeing you in action," Eddie chimed in. "I bet Ray that you'd wind up passed out on the table by the end of the evening."

"My money was on you passing out on the floor," Ray laughed.

"Sorry, boys," I tried to set them straight. "The free entertainment is over."

"Whoa! What happened to the party animal we used to know and love?" Eddie refused to back off.

"He ended up killing someone in a blackout and spending eleven years in jail," I snapped back.

Eddie and Ray were quiet. I was trying to figure out if they were more upset about what I did or that I wasn't going to put on a show for them.

"Listen guys, it's great to see you and catch up. But you've gotta understand that I haven't had a drink in over a decade and I don't plan on picking one up ever again."

I gave them the abbreviated version of my tale of woe and told them about my new life in recovery. Not another word was spoken about my lack of humor. As the evening wore on, we ended up talking about our long-term goals, and they expressed genuine concern about my lack of retirement plans.

"What are you going to do?" Eddie asked. I could tell that he was honestly worried.

"I'll deal with it when I get there." I brushed it off.

"You need a plan," Ray wouldn't let it go.

"I'll be dead by then anyway," I joked.

When they wouldn't let it go, I finally leaned over to them and said in a low voice, "Okay, you want to know my plan. I'm gonna rob a bank in Vermont and then come back to New York."

I could see the blood draining out of both their faces.

"Then, I'm going to rob another bank in Massachusetts and come back home. I'm going to keep on doing that every four months, hitting different states. I'll go to Connecticut, Jersey, and all the states in the Northeast. Once I hit all of them, I'll start back in Vermont all over again."

"What happens if you get caught?" Ray whispered.

After pausing for a moment, I burst out into a boisterous laugh. "You assholes really believed me!"

They both broke out in laughter and I could see them relax. "You may be sober, Richard—but you're still full of shit!" Ray bellowed as he slapped me on the back.

As the laughter died down, I got serious again. "Don't worry about me, guys. I'm not worried. As long as I'm doing the next right thing, I'll always get what I need."

On the way home that evening I got to thinking about what the next right thing was for me. I'd been in New York for fifteen months and felt that I had made the amends I needed to make. While it felt good to be closer to Kate, New York wasn't home to me anymore. Florida was. I decided to head back to Miami, but a few days later I discovered that the big boss of the universe had other plans for me.

Right before Christmas I got a call from Don, my buddy who came to speak at my banquet at Avon Park. He was taking a leap of faith by opening up an in-patient treatment facility, and he wanted me to help him get it up and running. Don explained that Butch had filled him in on my move into the treatment field. He was impressed with how I helped to launch other businesses in the past, and he knew I was a real workhorse. Ironically, his new facility was in Palm Beach County where I had been arrested. When I heard that, I knew it was an offer I couldn't refuse. It was the next right thing.

After celebrating the holidays with Kate and the rest of my family, I hopped into my six-year-old Oldsmobile and headed to Palm Beach Gardens. Don arranged for me to share an apartment with a couple of other transplanted New Yorkers who were going to work at the facility with me. I immediately felt as if I was being rewarded for doing the right thing when I pulled up to my new pad. It was a brand-new apartment complex with swimming pools, Jacuzzis, a gym, handball court, and even a small theater. The place was plush and I was living large.

After a couple of days of settling in, we opened for business on January 1 with three patients. I'd drive them to Don's outpatient offices, outside meetings, and the fitness center. I gave them the meds prescribed by their doctors and, for my own sanity, would check in on them at night and make sure that they were in bed with their TVs off. While I would occasionally run a group, I was basically a babysitter.

This went on for about six months until Mike, the new director, told me he didn't want me to drive the vans anymore. He wanted me to be a therapist. I was thrilled at the opportunity. Finally I could put to use everything I learned from running Go-Lab groups, working at the Pines, and from my personal experiences. I immediately signed up for night and weekend classes to get my certification in alcohol and drug therapy. In the meantime, a credentialed therapist signed off for me, and I would look at other therapists' files to learn how to write treatment plans. I felt like I was where I belonged.

Everything was falling into place, and it wasn't long before I found a new squeeze—Kate. Actually, she was an old one I knew from my Twelve-Step network. In typical fashion, things progressed quickly between us. She moved up from Miami to be closer to me and before I knew it I was living with her. Everything seemed to be falling into place. Kate even got season tickets for the Marlins, so we spent a lot of time together going to the games. The Marlins won the wild card that year, and we were lucky enough to go to the playoffs and the World Series.

The treatment facility grew in leaps and bounds. Within the first year we had so many patients that we needed to start renting out new places. We hit a couple bumps in the road at this stage, though, since many of our neighbors weren't keen on us bringing in a bunch of addicts to the community. For some reason, they weren't happy when one of our patients started wandering around trying to trade stolen steaks for vodka. The complaints kept causing headaches for our landlords, so we had to move from time to time. Eventually, we purchased part of a vacation complex on Singer Island and additional property in western Lake Worth.

In August 1997, Don brought in a new partner. Jack had an outpatient facility outside of Philly and could send us patients who weren't successful there because they needed in-patient care. Then, in a crazy twist of fate, we started getting law enforcement officers from a union rep in New Jersey. The first one who came failed, so I thought we wouldn't see any more of them, but I was wrong. The rep knew that it was the ex-cop who failed, not us, and he kept sending us more patients.

Ironically, most of these officers ended up in my group because I was the counselor who understood them. After all the years of my battling it out with Johnny Law because I was drinking, I ended up helping them with the same problem when I was sober. It wasn't easy at first. Countless arrests and eleven years in prison will inevitably result in a grudge toward law enforcement. Once I shook off the humongous chip on my shoulder, however, I was in a unique position to help them. I knew what they had to put up with: me! My years in the joint gave me the insight to understand why it was so hard for them to show any sign of weakness. In the world they lived in, vulnerability could get them killed. They couldn't admit that a lousy little powder could control them. They had to be macho to do their jobs. So they built up walls around themselves to survive. My job was to break them down and build them back up—in three weeks time. I would tell them, "For once in your life, bring that wall down. Don't save your face, save your ass. If you keep this up you're going to die, or you're going to screw up your life so badly you're going to wish you were dead."

The brutal scenes I witnessed in prison also helped me recognize that many of these patients were not only addicts, but trauma victims as well. They'd had to cut down bodies after people had hanged themselves. They'd been covered in blood after inmates had stabbed each other. They'd seen bodies thrown off tiers. Many had been physically attacked themselves. This pain had to be addressed along with their addiction.

Because I understood the needs and fears of police and corrections officers, I built up a reputation for my work with them. Our facility's Safety Officers Program got a lot of attention because a high percentage of our patients stayed in recovery long after they left. I even got on the cover of a treatment magazine. Union reps started sending us cops, corrections officers, and firefighters from all over the Northeast, and then they started coming in from Kentucky, Tennessee, and Illinois. We expanded our program to deal with other mental illnesses as well. It wasn't long before we had over a hundred patients at a time.

I had finally found a sense of peace. I wasn't hurting people anymore. I was helping them. It was fulfilling to watch people transform before my eyes. We had patients come in who couldn't stand up because they were suffering from neuropathy from drinking too much for too long. Three weeks later they were walking out the door with their heads held high. People would come in beaten down, filled with despair, and leave healthy and hopeful.

Not everyone recovered. Some patients thought they were bulletproof. They thought that they were too cool to be straight. They didn't understand that they were battling a life-threatening disease. Some of them never had to worry about detox again, though. They ended up overdosing in dilapidated buildings, wrapping their cars around trees, or saying farewell to their friends and family as their livers stopped functioning.

With every miraculous recovery and tragic death, I was reminded of how important it was for me to stay sober. Over the next few years, I had my ups and downs, but I knew that my higher power would do for me what I couldn't do for myself.

When I struggled with heart disease, dealt with Kate and me breaking up, and had to cope with not always succeeding at work, I was able to handle it because I knew there was a greater plan to the universe. Thanks to the Twelve-Step program, I had faith in myself and faith in life. The program did so much more for me than get me sober. It helped me be honest with myself and others. It reminded me to have character, not just be one. While I can say that prison saved my life, the Twelve-Step program saved my soul. Before I got sober, I didn't want to live but was afraid to die. Today I want to live, but I'm not afraid to die.

Right before Christmas in 2002, I received a letter from my daughter Katie. Along with the letter, she included the following lyrics to a song she wrote called "In My Life."

Wonderin' about your life, what ever brought you to this.
What was so bad in your life that ever made you do this.
Didn't you see how your life affected me.
Didn't you see without you I couldn't be free.

Oh, Daddy,
Because you hit your bottom, sunk down so deep and low,
I cried the tears for you Daddy, your love I craved to know.
I wish I could see the future, to know things would be all right.
If only I knew things sooner, I could have felt safer at night.
In my life I held you high.
In your world you just got by.
But that only lasted for so long.
Suddenly your right became my wrong.
You did the best with what you had;
Daddy you know I could never stay mad.

The world's been turning thousands of times since then.
You turned your world around now, you helped a lot of men.

Funny how things turn out.
Your life now downside up.
I hope you know I love you Daddy;
On you, I never gave up.

I'm so proud now of everything about you.
Isn't it amazing what one man can do:
To walk away from ego and greed,
To finally find what your life needs.
Life's too short for endless sorrow.
I hope today for others' new tomorrow.

In my life I held you high.
In your world you just got by.
But that only lasted for so long.
Suddenly your right became my wrong.
You did the best with what you had;
Daddy you know I could never stay mad.

You found your forgiveness, you made amends.
A rough row to hoe:
Your life had to follow this path.
Many lessons you had to know.

In my life I held you high.
In your world you just got by.
But that only lasted for so long.
Suddenly your right became my wrong.
You did the best with what you had;
Daddy you know I could never stay mad.

Afterword

ON THE STEAMY SUMMER MORNING OF JULY 5, 2007, I awoke before daybreak. Excited to catch the sunrise, I leaped out of bed to head to the beach. As I stood there alone, watching the waves gently washing upon the shore, I remembered that twenty-five years ago I was hiding in the dark. Today I was racing to see the dawn. As the sun illuminated the horizon, I said a prayer of gratitude for getting a chance to wake up to a new day.

About the Author

R ICHARD B. BROOM, BORN RICHARD B. TREMPER in 1946, grew up in Albany, New York. He graduated from Guilderland Central High School in 1963 and Hudson Valley Community College in 1970. He was honorably discharged from the U. S. Army in October 1968. The author has two daughters and now resides in Palm Beach Gardens, Florida, where he is a therapist at Behavioral Health of the Palm Beaches, an alcohol and drug treatment facility.

Memoir...

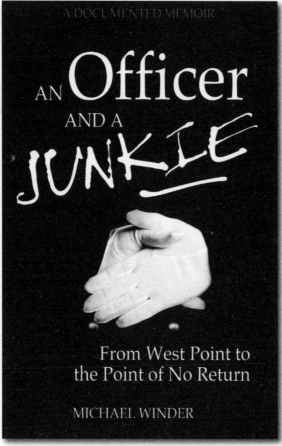

A DOCUMENTED MEMOIR

AN **Officer** AND A **JUNKIE**

From West Point to
the Point of No Return

MICHAEL WINDER

Code #639X • Paperback • $15.95

In *An Officer and A Junkie* From West Point to the Point of No Return, Michael Winder shares how he longed to be a part of America's elite—to stand in The Long Gray Line as an officer in the United States Army. But, before the end of his sophomore year, Winder buckled under pressure, and in search of an escape, he turned to alcohol and recreational drugs— eventually plummeting into debilitating and self-destructive abuse.
